THE S(

GOVERNORS'

YEARBOOK

2013

Adamson Publishing

Copyright © 2012 Adamson Publishing Ltd

Published by Adamson Publishing Ltd
8 The Moorings
Norwich NR3 3AX
☎ 01603 623336 fax 01603 624767
info@adamsonbooks.com
www.adamsonbooks.com

ISBN 978-0948543-68-5

British Library Cataloguing in Publication Data
A catalogue record for this book is available from the British Library

Cover design by Geoff Shirley
Cover photos: *from left* 1 and 4 supplied by Serco Education Bradford,
others from iStockphoto

Printed by Bell and Bain Ltd, Glasgow

Preface

School governors are normally typified as shadowy figures working behind the scenes, but this year they are likely to find themselves in an unaccustomed position in the limelight. Now so much else in our schools system has been subject to fierce scrutiny in the name of improving pupil outcomes, governance has increasingly come to attention as the possible key to raising standards. We have recently heard an ex Schools Minister argue that our current system of governance is unsuitable for schools today, the present Secretary of State claim that some governing bodies are Victorian in outlook and practice, and HM Chief Inspector of Schools state that governing bodies will be examined to see if they work to a high professional level.

All this is against a background of a hike in floor standards, more public testing of schools, an Ofsted vocabulary that no longer admits the term "satisfactory", new rules on governing body constitution and reform of the curriculum. With less support going to schools to meet their objectives, perhaps it is not surprising that the unpaid volunteers should be looked to to deliver the goods.

Yet none of this is really new for governors, nor should we shy away from the attendant responsibilities. Governors have been charged in law for 14 years with seeing that their schools attain high standards, and no governor worth their salt will have taken on the role for anything less than contributing to helping pupils fulfil their potential to its maximum.

The problem is that the debate often seems to be happening in an atmosphere of threat and retribution rather than reflection. The portrayal of governors has sometimes been caricature rather than characterisation, and a caricature at that which owes more to history than to the present day. Where there is little evidence about what makes for effective governance, opinions easily get formed by prejudice rather than fact. One of the realities that is often overlooked is that in face of the failure of governance in such important institutions as banking and the media, schools are getting quite a lot of it right.

The authors of this book aim to stick to information rather than supposition, and to concentrate on the practical rather than the hypothetical. We hope that over the course of this year there will be informed debate about what makes effective governing bodies and what reforms might be necessary to keep apace with a fast changing schools system. That way all governing bodies should be able to perform the outstanding job that must be the aim of all who volunteer.

STEPHEN ADAMSON
Editor

Contents

part one RECENT CHANGES AND CURRENT ISSUES

The year that was   8
Inspection ratchets up further *Steve Mansfield*   10
Reconstituting your governing body, or not
   Stephen Adamson   13
Partnership models for the current educational landscape
   Martin Lawrence   16
Governing in an academy *Phil Hand*   18
Governance and standards *Nicola Croke*   21
Pupil achievement – how do we measure up? *Vince Quayle* 24
Using the Pupil Premium *Felicity Taylor*   26
Policies: a cut too far? *Michele Robbins*   28
Performance management and capability *David Marriott*   31
More or less, reforms to funding *Harriet Manson*   34
Completing the Schools Financial Value Standard
   Stephen Adamson   36
Governor responsibilities on pupil behaviour *David Marriott* 38
Governing the curriculum *Sue Platt*   41
Bringing computing back into schools
   Neil Collins and Simon Peyton-Jones   43
What schools have to publish   44
New tunes for Wales *Allan Tait*   45
Appointing headteachers *Martin Pounce*   47
Support for chairs from the National College
   David Marriott   49
New rules on exclusion *Stephen Adamson*   51
Learning the lessons about safeguarding children
   Michele Robbins   53
The governors' national association *Stephen Adamson*   56
In brief   58

part two PLANNING AND RESOURCES

The governing body   60
Annual workplan   62
Essential documents   67
Compliance with statutory regulations   70
School types   73
How academies differ from maintained schools   75
Ofsted's key characteristics of outstanding governing bodies   76
Twenty key questions   78
The floor standards   79
Governance in Wales   80
The National Curriculum   81
Information sources   82
Common terms, abbreviations and acronyms   89
Useful addresses   93
Who's Who in Education   95

Index   96

part one

RECENT CHANGES
AND CURRENT
ISSUES

2013

The year that was

September 2011
∗ Headteachers' union the NAHT votes for the first time in favour of strike action, in a proposal to join with other unions in a mass day of action against public service pension changes.

October
∗ The Institute for Fiscal Studies calculates that educational spending is to fall 14.4 percent between 2010–11 and 2014-15, but that schools funding is one of the least badly affected areas.
∗ Government accedes to House of Lords rejection of its move to abolish the statutory duty on schools to cooperate with local authority and other providers on child welfare.
∗ Research finds that, contrary to general supposition, children from highly disadvantaged backgrounds do not suffer from lack of aspiration.

November
∗ Diplomas for 14–19-year-olds are effectively killed off when three major exam boards decide to cease offering the qualification.
∗ The Education Act 2011 comes into law.
∗ Thousands of schools close in widespread industrial day of action on public service pensions.

December
∗ Two chief examiners are suspended after claims that they tipped schools off as to the questions likely to be asked in some GCSEs.
∗ National Curriculum review panel recommends that history, geography and modern foreign languages become compulsory for all children in Key Stages 2 and 4.

January 2012
∗ Sir Michael Wilshaw, previously principal of Mossbourne Academy in Hackney, becomes HM Chief Inspector of Schools (HMCI).
∗ DfE amends model funding agreement for academies and Free Schools to prevent schools being set up that will teach creationism as science (though it can be taught under RE).

February
∗ HMCI announces proposed changes to the new Ofsted framework for inspecting schools that will replace the "satisfactory" grade and open the way for schools repeatedly graded less than good to be put in special measures.
∗ Lord Knight, former Schools Minister under the Labour government,

publishes article that argues for radical reform of school governance, including paying chairs of governing bodies, on the grounds that currently too many governing bodies are not good enough.

✳ Research finds that slightly more pupils with English as an additional language get A*–C GCSE grades than native English speakers.

March

✳ The DfE removes its recommended times for the amount of homework that should be set for each year group.

✳ Government introduces a requirement that every school in receipt of Pupil Premium funding should publish details of how much it receives, what has been done with it and what it proposes to do in future.

✳ New Early Years Foundation Stage curriculum published, to come into force from September 2012. It is shorter and simpler than previous curricula, and introduces a new assessment for two-year-olds.

✳ Government announces that no changes will be made to national funding formulas until 2015 at the earliest, despite original intentions to introduce changes in 2013-14. However, changes are made to the rules determining what criteria local authorities can use in funding schools.

April

✳ Taylor Report, on school attendance, published, including a proposal to remove the concept that term-time holidays can be acceptable.

May

✳ The Schools Network, previously the Specialist Schools and Academies Trust, goes into administration with substantial debts.

✳ Details of Priority Schools Building Programme announced, listing which schools will receive government funding for rebuilding or refurbishment.

June

✳ Draft new primary curriculum published for English, maths and science, containing prescriptions on the teaching of reading and the removal of National Curriculum "levels".

✳ Secretary of State for Education confirms that he is planning to reform the public exam system and is reported as believing that new exams should look more like the old O levels.

July

✳ Secretary of State for Education says that while some governing bodies do an excellent job, others have sprawling committees and are blighted by "local worthies" who are in it only for the status.

✳ TES and NGA survey of school governors find that only 21 percent approve of the Coalition's performance, as opposed to 40 percent a year previously.

Inspection ratchets up further

The latest changes in inspection continue the direction of travel inherent in the framework instituted in January 2012. There are valuable lessons for all schools from the experiences of those inspected since it started.

Shortly after a new inspection framework came into effect at the beginning of 2012, a new HM Chief Inspector of Schools, Sir Michael Wilshaw, was appointed, who almost immediately announced that he wanted to make further changes. Although some of his suggestions have been moderated in response to consultations, there are still radical changes in the notice period and the grading of level 3.

The September 2012 changes

In September the overall judgement for grade 3 ceased to be "satisfactory" and became "requires improvement". The old term had in any event become redundant, as government and Ofsted had been openly stating for some time, in defiance of meaning, that "satisfactory is not good enough". However, a school graded 3 does not fall into the category of "causing concern" – that remains solely for grade 4.

The aim behind this change is to prevent schools coasting at only a moderate level. Schools given a grade 3 will be monitored and re-inspected within two years. If they remain at the same level for the next two inspections – i.e. for a total of four years – they will normally be put in special measures. There is some discretion for the lead inspector, but special measures will be the norm other than in exceptional circumstances, such as if a new headteacher has recently been appointed and has already started to improve the school.

Grade 4 continues to be divided into two sub-categories, the lower being requiring "special measures". Being given a "notice to improve" becomes exhibiting "serious weaknesses". Both sub-categories are for schools that inspectors believe are inadequate, but in those with "serious weaknesses" they will have seen evidence that persuades them that the leadership team has the capacity to improve the school.

The notice period for inspection has been reduced to half a day. Your headteacher will normally be phoned after noon on the last working day before the inspection is to begin. This is designed to allow them to rearrange their diaries if necessary, to enable the school to alert parents so that they can register their opinions of the school overnight on Parent View, and to allow the governing body to ensure that a suitable member (usually but not necessarily the chair) to be present to meet the inspector(s). Bear in mind, though, that the Chief Inspector still has the power to authorise a no-notice inspection if he considers it necessary.

Two other proposals had caused concern during the consultation period. The first was the requirement of the school to provide inspectors with staff performance management reports. It was feared that this would compromise the appraisal process, which only works properly if staff can freely admit to any shortcomings that need professional development. Ofsted have responded to this concern by still requiring the reports, but agreeing that these should be anonymised, so as not to expose individuals. The aim of this is to allow inspectors to see whether the way the leadership conducts performance management impacts on pupil performance.

The second relates to the judgement of "outstanding". This will only be given to schools where teaching is judged to be outstanding. However, to achieve this it is not necessary for every lesson observed by inspectors to be outstanding; they will make an overall judgement based on everything that they have seen.

Governors
Since January 2012 the quality of governance has been recorded in reports, but it does not receive a formal grading. This has not changed.

However, under the current framework governance has been placed more centrally in school improvement, and the role of governors is given greater prominence than before. Governors are regarded as an active part of the leadership. The FAQs issued by Ofsted when announcing the changes to the framework in May 2012 (www.ofsted.gov.uk/resources/responses-ofsteds-consultation-good-education-for-all) yoke governors and school leaders together in discussing schools' ability to improve (such as in the statement on schools with serious weaknessess on page 55).

Governors continue to be seen by the inspectors, normally on the second morning of the inspection. The inspector concerned will ask for the chair, but the governing body can allocate another governor if it wishes. You can also ask for more than one governor to attend the meeting; the inspector should not refuse this. The chair will also be invited to the feedback session with the senior leadership team at the end of the inspection.

At the morning meeting the inspector should already have formed a view of the school and will have an idea of the overall judgement that the team is considering making. Inevitably, there is an element for the governor of being judged, and different inspectors will have their own approaches to handling the meeting, but it is also an opportunity for the governor to put their own view and to talk about the work that the governing body has been doing to move the school forward. Given that inspectors' judgements depend heavily on the leadership team persuading them that they have an accurate view of where the school stands and what to do about it, impressing the inspectors of the clarity of the governing body's own vision can only help secure a satisfactory outcome.

Other lessons from the first two terms
Though significant, the September changes only develop school inspection

on the lines it was following in the previous months. In particular, shortening the preparation time for schools has been designed to ensure inspectors see the school on a typical day. They had already been trying to ascertain how typical what they observed was, for example, by asking pupils about whether the behaviour in a lesson was normal.

Although Ofsted's Self Evaluation Form for schools was removed in 2011, inspectors still expect schools to conduct their own self-evaluation, and will examine whatever document the school uses before they carry out their visit. They will look for evidence that the leadership has an accurate picture of the school and what action it needs. Although some governors have reported that the inspection of their school was a positive process, with inspectors underlining the judgement that governors and leaders had themselves made of the school, other governors have reported more negative experiences, with inspectors appearing to have made up their minds about the school before they came, and ignoring evidence that ran counter to this pre-judgement.

Whatever your view of the inspector's judgements, the process should be open. Inspectors have been sharing their views with the headteacher during the conduct of the inspection, in particular at the feedback meeting with the head at the end of the first day. With the governor's meeting early on the second day, the head can share this report with the chair so that they are prepared.

There is, however, a relentlessness to the new framework which has led to some complaints that the approach is punitive. The contextual value added measures in RAISEonline data have already been removed, on the grounds that they provided excuses for poor work by schools. The new designation of grade 3 is a further intensification of the spotlight on school standards, with a lot of schools (some 38 percent having been graded "satisfactory" in 2010–11) now to be judged as performing poorly. Ofsted argue that nothing less than good should be acceptable; critics of the new framework say that it is setting up schools to fail.

There has been less emphasis on compliance, and governors generally can expect not to be subjected to a lot of questions about their statutory policies, providing that there is evidence in the minutes of governors' meetings (which inspectors ask to see) of their having established these. This is not to say that compliance has disappeared altogether, and schools will still need to show that they provide adequate safeguarding for children and conduct the proper checks on staff.

The four areas of inspection – pupil achievement, quality of teaching, standards of behaviour and quality of leadership – should be entrenched in the school's self-evaluation processes. The new changes do nothing to change these four fundamentals, but governors may feel that the task of achieving high standards has been made that bit harder and the results of failing to do so that bit more severe.

STEVE MANSFIELD

Reconstituting your governing body, or not

The long-heralded powers to change the constitution of the governing body came into effect at the beginning of this school year. They give governing bodies that want it the power to appoint most of their members.

The new rules on governing body constitutions are contained in *The School Governance (Constitution) (England) Regulations 2012*, which came into force on 1 September 2012 (on www.legislation.gov.uk/uksi/2012/1034/schedule/1/made). These rules contain much less prescription about who can sit on a governing body than previous regulations, and also allow for smaller governing bodies.

The new regulations apply only to maintained schools. All governing bodies of maintained schools formed after 1 September 2012 will have to follow them. Existing governing bodies can reconstitute under the new regulations, but may keep their existing constitution if they wish.

Numbers and types of governor under the new regulations

The only constraint on **size** is that the governing body must have a minimum of seven members. There is no upper limit.

There must be a minimum of two elected **parent governors**. The governing body may choose to have more elected parent governors, or may co-opt some parents as governors.

The **headteacher** has a right to a place on the governing body. He or she may waive that right, but the place remains open to them at any time if they later change their mind.

One governor must be elected by **the staff**. The staff governor can be a teacher or a member of the support staff.

The term "**local authority governor**" has been reinstated. There is one place for a governor appointed by the local authority (LA). The governing body may determine the skills that it requires of such a governor before an appointment is made. If it does not consider that the person nominated by the LA meets the eligibility criteria, it can refuse to appoint them. The LA may then nominate other people for consideration. Members of staff cannot be appointed as LA governors.

The old term "**co-opted governor**" replaces "community governor". The governing body can appoint as many of these as it wishes. Some may be members of the school's staff (in addition to the elected staff governor), but the total of staff members – including the staff governor and the headteacher – is limited to a maximum of one third of the governing body.

There is no separate category of **sponsor governors**. The governing body may, if it wishes, include people suggested by a sponsor among the co-opted governors.

All governing bodies may appoint **associate members**, as before.

The position is more complicated with **foundation and voluntary schools**, where the proportion of foundation/partnership governors is protected. In foundation schools that do not have a foundation and in voluntary controlled schools, there must be a minimum of two partnership/foundation governors, but the total number must not exceed a quarter of the governing body. In foundation schools that do have a foundation but which are not trust schools the foundation governors must number at least two and not make up more than 45 percent of the entire governing body. In trust schools ("qualifying foundation schools") and voluntary aided schools the total number of foundation governors should outnumber all the other governors by two.

Appointing and removing governors

The responsibility for **elections** of parent and staff governors rests with the "appropriate authority", which is the LA for community, maintained nursery and voluntary controlled schools, and the governing body for a voluntary aided or foundation school. This responsibility may be delegated to the headteacher. Similar rules to the previous ones apply to parental elections, including the power to appoint if there are not enough candidates, except that it is specified that parents must be able to vote in elections by post, and that the governing body may also permit electronic voting.

There is no change in the rules over the **term of office**. The term is four years (except for the headteacher), unless the governing body agrees a shorter one for a particular category of governor. If this happens the term and category must be specified in the instrument of government.

Co-opted governors (including appointed parent governors) and partnership governors may be **removed** by a vote of the governing body. Elected governors still cannot be removed, but as most governors in a reconstituted governing body will be co-opted, this will give governing bodies more power to act over governors who do not perform.

Considering reconstitution

If you are happy with the size and make-up of your current governing body, do not have great difficulty in appointing governors, and consider that the present constitution is appropriate for the work you have to do, you will probably not want to reconstitute. However, if you think that you do not have the range of skills on the governing body that you need, that you have too many or too few governors, or that certain categories of governor are always difficult to fill, you may want to consider reconstituting.

However, if you have a temporary difficulty in filling a vacancy or just wish to lose some of your current governors, reconstituting may be tempting but might not be the right solution. Reconstitution should not be seen as a quick fix but as a way of giving the governing body a structure that will serve it for a number of years (though you can review the new constitution at any time).

The key thing is to consider the work that the governing body has to do and the people that it needs in order to do them. This will relate to the aims and ethos of the school. Reconstituting allows governing bodies to be more skills-based, whereas the old constitution is based upon representing stakeholders. The questions you could ask could include:

- Is it a strength of our school that is rooted in the community?
- Do we benefit from having a strong parent presence on the governing body?
- Are we able to provide the challenge and support to the senior leadership team that is needed to move the school on?
- Are we always focused on our strategic role?
- Are our meetings always effective?
- Do we have enough committees to do our work, and enough people to serve on them?

If the answer to all these questions is "yes", then your present constitution is serving the school well, but if you record a couple of "noes", then you should consider changing the constitution, especially if one of the "noes" was to the third question.

If you do reconstitute you should consider how to use your greater powers of co-option. What skills do you want to add to the governing body? Remember that the role of the governing body is strategic, and that, for example, though you need some governors with a good grasp of finance, your role is not to appoint an accountant to administer the school's budget. On the other hand, it can only strengthen the governing body if you appoint people who can understand the school's key data, and who can provide appropriate challenge to the senior leadership team.

The process of changing

A governing body can consider adopting a new instrument of government at any time. The decision has to be made by resolution of the entire governing body and cannot be delegated.

The governing body must notify the LA of the intended change, together with its reasons for making them. A foundation or voluntary school must first secure the agreement of the foundation governors and, where applicable, of the trustees, the diocesan authority, or other appropriate religious body.

If the old governing body had more members in any category than are specified for the new one and not enough of the surplus is eliminated by people volunteering to stand down, those in that category who have been on the governing body the shortest period of time will be required to resign. In the event of there being more people of equal seniority than are required to resign, the resignations must be determined by lot.

STEPHEN ADAMSON

Partnership models for the current education landscape

This a challenging time for governing bodies in considering their school's future. Whatever the type of your school, partnerships with other schools are likely to be an essential part of your plans.

Governing bodies are simultaneously being encouraged to consider the greater freedoms offered by academy status while also focusing on improving teaching in their schools through school-to-school support. Whether you already have academy status, have decided against or are yet to consider, you should be looking at whether you have the right model of leadership and governance to secure your school's future. This should include exploring how best to work with neighbouring schools, clusters or chains of schools.

The background to these decisions is tight budgets, difficulties in recruiting outstanding headteachers, and an increased emphasis on governing body accountability for school performance. All are important factors in schools' longer-term strategic planning.

Staying alone as a single school is becoming more challenging for a lot of schools, especially smaller ones. Many headteachers are feeling vulnerable in the light of the continual raising of the bar on pupil outcomes. Your local authority has changed from supplier of services and a support mechanism to a more detached risk manager with significantly reduced resources. If your school is feeling these pressures you may need to consider how long it can sustain its single status.

Considering partnership options

Collaboration between schools has been encouraged for a decade now, either informally or through federation. **Collaborative partnerships** offer an opportunity to share staffing costs, resources, experiences and ideas, good practice and economies of scale. In **hard federations** you get a single governing body, and often a single headteacher, responsible for a number of schools. Federations already have a track record of delivering stronger leadership and improved outcomes for children. For details on forming a hard federation, go to www.education.gov.uk>Schools>Leadership and governance >Collaborations and federations.

Some schools that wanted to work closely together but without losing a strong relationship with a local authority or their co-operative democratic values have formed a **co-operative trust**. This is a grouping of maintained schools that is supported by a foundation trust. It enables the schools to work closely together while keeping their separate governing bodies and autonomy. The co-operative school movement has grown significantly, with 100 such trusts currently, and is an alternative to academy chains. A guide published by the DCSF in 2009, *Co-operative Schools, Making a Difference* has been kept available on the DfE website, under Publications, as it is still relevant. Information is also given by the Schools Cooperative Society on www.co-operativeschools.coop.

One way of bringing together maintained schools and academies to provide school-to-school support is through the current development of **teaching school alliances**. Only coming into existence in July 2011, they are now beginning to play a leading role in providing initial teacher training and in providing guidance for experienced teachers. To become a teaching school a school or academy has to have been designated as having outstanding teaching. It then forms an alliance with other schools so that they can benefit from professional development provided by the teaching school for their leaders and teachers. These alliances can cross sectors and local authority boundaries.

Teaching school programmes are being co-ordinated by the National College. If it is not already in one, your school is quite likely soon to have the opportunity to join such an alliance.

Academy partnerships or chains

Both the Secretary of State for Education and the Chief Inspector for Schools are promoting the development of academy partnerships and chains, in the belief that they provide sustainable models of governance. If there are problems in leadership and governance in a particular school, the partnership can provide, within a legal framework, the necessary school-to-school support. These arrangements require powers and accountability to be shared across a number of schools. There are a few models available, which each offer a differing degree of local control.

In a **multi-academy trust** one trust governs a group of schools. Each school will have a local advisory body, which the trust can constitute as a local governing body to which certain functions can be delegated, though it may choose not to delegate any. While this will be likely to reduce local decision-making, the school has the security of working within a formalised group.

An **umbrella academy trust** model allows schools of different categories, such as voluntary aided and voluntary controlled schools, to form a legal partnership. The schools can nominate representatives to sit on an umbrella trust to oversee the leadership and governance of the group, but they keep their own governing bodies. Individual schools converting as **single academy trusts** can alternatively agree to work within a collaborative partnership, with no shared trust or formalised governance structure, all the schools jointly determining the nature of the academy partnership.

Information on these is on the DfE's website, www.education.gov.uk<Schools<Leadership and governance<Types of schools.

MARTIN LAWRENCE

Governing in an academy

It's often said that governing an academy is the same as governing a maintained school, but there can be significant differences and academy governors need to know just what powers they have.

Academy governance can be very confusing. Governance is the aspect of school life that changes most when a school converts to being an academy. The shift from School Government Regulations into company law, and the opportunity schools have to develop unique governance arrangements within their articles of association, make for a varied landscape. One commentator (Bridget Sinclair, chair of NCOGS) put it thus: "One important feature seems to be that each model of school carries with it its own evolving book of rules and those governors and leaders in these new integrated structures are finding their own way often on a case-by-case basis. Each academy model requires a unique model of governance, and each academy is bound by potentially unique articles of associations and funding agreements."

For a start, there are three main models of academy governance: a single academy, a multi-academy chain/trust and an umbrella trust (see page 17 for details). Many other variations of academy partnerships exist, but these three are the most common.

Directors and local committees

So let's get some of the terminology right at the outset. In maintained schools, a governing body is a statutory body with statutory powers. Under the original legislation in the 1986 Education Act and the 1988 Education Reform Act, a governing body is set up with the legal responsibility to receive the budget, hire and fire the staff, and oversee the school. While the local authority is a real presence in terms of keeping a watchful eye on standards, admissions, exclusions and the budget, "local management of schools" (from the 1988 Act) means that it is the governing body, not the local authority, that runs the school.

In an academy, the statutory body is the board of directors (also known as "trustees"), and it is the directors who exercise the statutory powers (Model Articles of Association (Multi Academy), Article 93). These should not be confused with the "members", a (usually) smaller group with the responsibility to steer the overall ethos and values of the school and appoint or remove governors. Members can be and often are also directors.

In a single academy, the directors and the governors are the same people. In a multi-academy model, the terms "governor" and "director" are kept entirely separate. The governance absolutely sits with the directors, and the board of directors is made up of roles traditionally associated with governance – parent directors, staff directors, co-opted directors, etc. This raises the questions of the place of governors in a multi-academy trust.

In such a trust, the directors can appoint committees in the individual schools, and most do so. Different chains give different names to these. Oasis Community Learning, a multi-academy sponsor overseeing 14 academies, calls the local committee in any of its academies the "Academy Council". At the time of writing the Catholic Archdiocese of Birmingham is planning to use the term "Academy Committee". Other chains will use different terminology.

The Model Articles of Association for multi-academies use the term "Local Governing Body", but members of such a body are not actually governors at all in the sense of the 1986 Act. The board of directors can empower such a committee through delegation, but there is no statutory tenure for a local governing body, which can be disbanded at any time by the directors.

This does cause a problem, because in multi-academy chains people are being appointed as members of a local governing body; they are told they are governors; they think they are governors; they attend governor training; but they are not part of a real governing body in the accepted sense of the term.

This is not necessarily a bad way of running things. Many people become governors because they want to visit the school, discuss school improvement, bring support and challenge to the head and do some strategic thinking about the future. These are all possible in the multi-academy model if the board of directors delegates these responsibilities to the local group. Indeed, in some chains the sheer number of academies makes it impossible for the directors to fulfil these roles. In addition, members of the local group may well not want the statutory responsibilities – pupil discipline committees, grievance and staff dismissal panels. The directors can handle all that.

The use of the term "Local Governing Body" does, nevertheless, suggest a shift of thinking about school governance on the part of central government. Is a governing body no longer expected to carry statutory powers? The most important thing, however, is that people who join such local boards are clear about their status and tenure, and how the statutory aspects of governance in the academy chain work.

One sensible use of these local committees is the election of parent directors to the board. There must be two parent directors for every ten academies in a multi-academy chain, and those parents elected to the local committee through a process determined by the board of directors elect parent directors from among their number.

Issues for academy governors

There are two other significant issues facing governors in academies.

First, there is a real change in culture from being a school governor to becoming both a company director and a charity trustee. Governors and directors of academies are registered as directors at Companies' House, and become trustees of a charitable trust with exempt charity status.

(However, they are not registered with or directly regulated by the Charity Commission, but rather by the DfE.) All the directors are trustees, not just the members.

There is also some debate about an individual governor's personal liability. Traditionally governors of maintained schools have been reassured that they carry no personal liability when acting in good faith. In an academy, governors purchase indemnity insurance. There are certain things this insurance cannot cover. These are any act or omission which the governors "knew to be a breach of trust or breach of duty"; or which was committed by the governors "in reckless disregard" of whether it was a breach of trust or breach of duty, and the costs of any "unsuccessful defence to a criminal prosecution" brought against the governors in their capacity as directors of the Academy Trust (quotes from article 6.3 of both model Articles of Association).

Secondly, there is a sharper than ever focus by central government and Ofsted on the importance of effective governance as schools become more independent. Local authorities have come in for a fair amount of criticism, but one thing they did well was act as a watchdog over standards and budgets, and if things were looking worrying they would first raise concerns and then intervene, sometimes using statutory powers. Who will do this in an academy structure?

Clearly the governors of an academy must obtain advice from outside the school. In an academy chain this may be immediately available from within the resources of the trust, but a single academy must buy this in. Of critical importance is that such external advice is commissioned by and reports to the governing body, rather than the principal (this is good advice for maintained schools as well). Exercising accountability has always been a difficult task, but governors must get better at it, and Ofsted will certainly scrutinise it.

Clearly over the next year school and academy governance will come under a great deal of scrutiny. There will be different pressures in this new world of independence. Some academy structures may need adjustment, and some changes to the rules may come. If the focus of governors in academies and all schools remains firmly on school improvement, standards and quality of provision, calling on the right help from partners outside the academy, things are likely to improve for all our children.

PHIL HAND

The Ofsted view

"Governors also need to keep up to date with their own training and development. It is particularly important that heads and academy principals find ways to ensure this happens when local authorities may be cutting such training because of financial constraints."

Sir Michael Wilshaw, HMCI, to the NGA Policy Conference, June 2012

Governance and standards

Governors need to use the levers at their disposal to fulfil their crucial responsibility for pupil achievement.

The heat on the grill now comes from both sides. On the one there is Ofsted inspection, with its narrower focus on the pupil achievement and the quality of teaching, and the other less support to governing bodies in achieving school improvement. Yet governing bodies, more than ever before, are being held to account for their school's standards.

The responsibility is far from new. The flagship educational legislation of Tony Blair's government, The School Standards and Framework Act, stated back in 1998: "The governing body shall conduct the school with a view to promoting high standards of educational achievement at the school." Through the many Educational Acts that have followed, this principle has not been removed or amended.

However, governing bodies do not have hands-on control of their schools. They do not even go into schools to check up on how well teachers are doing. So how can they exert influence on this key function?

The answer is that you don't have to have hands-on contact if you have a machinery for doing things, and governing bodies have various levers at their disposal to affect change further down the system. There are five main ones:

1. Use of school self-evaluation and planning
2. Reading data
3. Setting targets
4. Performance management
5. Use of resources

School self-evaluation and planning

Self-evaluation and strategic planning feed into each other. Planning for the future should start with appraisal of what you are doing now and how effective it is, while monitoring and evaluation have to be built on knowledge of what your aims were in the past. In the process of the monitoring and evaluation you are also holding the school to account, and in relation to self-appraisal, you are acknowledging your own accountability too.

Whatever document you are using for self-evaluation (see page 12) it is the most powerful tool that you have. Self-evaluation is at the core of inspection, with inspectors looking to see if the school knows its own strengths and weaknesses and is acting appropriately on the evidence. But it is not just a document for inspectors, it is for regular use by the governing body in its conversations with the school's leadership team. Different parts of the self-evaluation document may be handled by different committees of the governing body, but all governors should be aware of the key issues identified. Is there, for example, a weakness in reading, underperformance by children with SEN, poor results in Modern Languages?

Self-evaluation should identify both the school's strengths and weaknesses. You can celebrate the strengths, but the key is to identify what can be learned from them in addressing those areas that need improvement, and to ensure they do not decline through being taken for granted. What the school intends to do about both is the job of the school development plan (SDP). If the self-evaluation document identifies where we are on the map, the SDP shows both what we see as our destination and how we are going to get there.

The conduct of self-evaluation is basically a job for the senior leadership team, but the governing body should have discussed key points with them before work begins, and should study, interrogate and ultimately agree the document. In a sense it is never finalised as it will change as things happen during the school year, but at least once a year the governing body should formally approve it. The SDP will be more detailed and operational, and hence is the preserve of the teaching staff, but the governing body should know of its contents, be assured that it addresses the school's needs and also agree it.

Reading data

Schools have more data about themselves than ever before. A lot of this is at the level of the individual child, and hence is not appropriate for the governing body, but there is higher-level data that is. Chief of these is RAISEonline (see pages 24–5)

Data is the key to self-evaluation – anything else is subjective. Sometimes you have to use the subjective – a visit to the school will tell you just accurately whether it is a happy place, as will the results of a pupil questionnaire. But for most of the time the key information is factual. The data available will not just show the headline figures – the number of children reaching level 4 in their Key Stage SATS or the numbers achieving five A*s-Cs at GCSE – but will also give information about specific groups. It's this that provides the picture of what is really going on. If the SATS mathematics results were below expectations, this might have been to disappointing performance by the boys, the children with EAL, or those identified as gifted and talented, for example.

As governors you need to know, and you also need to ask the right questions. To follow the example given, if you are told that the results were poor because of the high number of pupils with SEN, then had the pupil profile changed during the two years since the targets were set? If not, then something else had happened to account for the underachievement. Were the results of pupils with SEN worse in maths than in English? The point of asking challenging question is not to try to trip the senior leadership up, but to help identify for the benefit of all what is going on behind the headline figures.

Target-setting

The legal requirement to set targets for performance at Key Stage 2 and Key Stage 4 has been removed. While it is true that overzealous pursuit of targets can lead to concentration on only a few areas, and can produce "teaching to targets" that is skewed in favour of passing exams, nevertheless schools need firm targets in order to measure progress. Moreover, while removing one requirement the government has produced others: the floor standards for both primary and secondary schools (see page 79) and the English Baccalaureate for secondary schools.

Most maintained schools still set Key Stage 2 or Key Stage 4 targets, if only because these are the areas in which the school is judged. But other targets can be agreed with the SLT, for specific groups of pupils. These should appear in the SDP. Such targets can help the governing body in pursuit of raising standards, as teachers can report on overall progress during the timescale set, based on the pupil-specific data they receive.

Performance management

Although it is the headteacher's job to conduct the performance management of the senior staff and delegate the rest to line managers (or in very small schools to performance manage all the staff themselves), that of the headteacher rests with the governing body.

The headteacher's appraisal should relate two what school-self evaluation has identified as the school's needs. In setting the two or three objectives for the head, the governors entrusted with this job are setting the priorities for the school (any targets for the head's own CPD will, of course, be personal). It used to be compulsory to include an objective that related to pupil progress; governors are now free to set whatever types of objective they consider appropriate, but given the centrality of pupil progress to what the school is doing, it is unlikely that you would not want to set an objective that relates to it.

Use of resources

Lastly, governing bodies control the school's purse. Budget setting should be related to the SDP. Where improvement is needed, there is likely to be some need for some money, whether it is on curriculum resources, ICT, deployment of teaching assistants or CPD for teachers. Although in setting the budgets you will just be dealing with the main budget lines and not dictating where every pound goes, if you allow extra under one of these headings to meet a particular need, it is part of the monitoring process to ask whether the funds have been spent as anticipated, and what outcomes they are producing.

Even if money is tight in your school, how you set the budget reflects your priorities – perhaps even more so. As with much of school governance, identifying priorities and monitoring how they are followed up are key tasks. In the end these results convert into educational standards.

NICOLA CROKE

Pupil achievement – how do we measure up?

What data should governors receive, and how should they use it?

The very first page of the latest *Guide to the Law* makes it clear that governing bodies must find ways of delegating more of their statutory duties to headteachers, to allow themselves to focus on "school performance", in other words on improving pupil outcomes. We also now have a more targeted Ofsted inspection framework, which reduced the number of inspection judgements from over 30 to just four (plus overall effectiveness). And the first judgement? Not surprisingly, Pupil Achievement.

To hold their school properly to account for its performance, governors have access to a diverse range of reports from heads and teachers, Ofsted inspectors and other external professionals. However, for a balanced understanding of their judgements, you also need an insight into the objective evidence they consider – the measurable data which allows comparison between schools, pupil groups, cohorts and subjects.

It is unrealistic to expect every governor to be able to analyse a RAISEonline report, but all members of a governing body should be aware of the key role of hard data in the school self-evaluation process, in order to understand the conclusions of the head and senior leadership team when they report on pupil attainment and progress. Alongside this overview, each school would benefit from having two or three governors (such as some of those on a Performance and Standards committee), who are trained in and familiar with the terminology and analyses in RAISEonline, Fischer Family Trust (FFT), and similar data reports.

The reason for this level of governor engagement is not to "second guess" the evaluations received from the professionals, but rather to provide the corporate governing body with an extra perspective into the evidence base used by them to reach their conclusions. Without an appropriate level of knowledge, you can neither act as a worthwhile sounding board for the head, nor effectively challenge and hold the school to account for its pupil achievement.

Attainment, progress and achievement

In its regular monitoring programme, each governing body needs to consider pupils' measurable attainment and progress, but also to evaluate achievement – are your pupils progressing as well as they should? What could you do to help them achieve more? Looking beyond the "average of an average", how well are different groups of pupils learning? Which groups in your school are vulnerable to underperformance compared to their local peers and their national counterparts? How do you compare with middle performing schools (50th percentile, shown in the FFT "B" estimates) and with higher performing schools (25th percentile, FFT "D" estimates)? The answers to these questions will inform your self-evaluation and help determine your school improvement priorities.

However, there are limitations in this use of performance data – small sample sizes and confidential pupil background issues mean that data often prompts questions rather than providing ready-made answers. And the inspection framework requires schools to demonstrate the achievement of pupils currently in the school, so you need data which – unlike RAISEonline – sheds light on year groups other than primary year 6 or the GCSE year. So you need to know how your school uses its own termly tracking of the attainment and progress of every year group, and how it intervenes in cases of emerging underperformance.

Puncturing the myths

There are some enticing myths around school performance data:

- "It was a difficult cohort" – is this rationale applied consistently to higher- as well as lower-than-usual performance?
- "Catch up" – do pupils who have made poor progress in one year really catch up in the next class? If so, what did we originally think they would learn in the following year?
- "My headteacher doesn't want governors to see this data" – isn't it more likely that most heads simply don't want governors to misinterpret it? A core of trained governors would resolve this.
- "The main purpose of data is to highlight problems" – RAISEonline, FFT and schools' internal tracking also provide evidence of strengths.

So how can governors obtain school performance data? Every governing body should regularly receive the school's professional evaluation, summarising the key implications of RAISEonline, perhaps of some FFT analyses, and of the school's internal tracking. This can be presented by the head or another member of staff at a governing body meeting, and potentially in more depth at a committee meeting. Governors can also access directly their online RAISEonline Summary report (which contains no confidential information on individual pupils), through a governors' password provided by the school. However a simpler method is to ask the school to provide an electronic copy of the report.

Heads and staff use measurable performance data to monitor how well pupils are achieving, and Ofsted inspectors look for evidence of this. If governing bodies are to hold schools effectively to account for pupils' achievement, they need a shared understanding of how they and their leadership team partners might respond to the questions raised of pupil attainment and progress.

For further information see "Data" on page 84.

VINCE QUAYLE

Using the Pupil Premium

All schools, including academies, in receipt of the Pupil Premium are expected to use it to help disadvantaged children and are now required to show how they do this.

The Pupil Premium is an extra payment, funded by the DfE, available to all schools. Its aim is to help schools to compensate for the educational disadvantage that can be suffered by children from poorer families. The premium was introduced in the financial year beginning April 2011. Funded by a specific grant from the DfE, local authorities distribute it to schools on the basis of the number of pupils eligible for free school meals (FSM). It is also given for children who have been in care continuously for more than six months. The amount per pupil was £488 in 2011-12 but has gone up to £600 for 2012-13.

Although FSM may be an imperfect benchmark for poverty and deprivation, it is generally held to be the best simple indicator of need. In this context it is significant that the distribution of the premium is based not on those claiming free school meals but on those known to be eligible for them. This was extended in 2012-3 to cover all children who have been eligible for FSM at any time in the last six years, even if they are no longer so.

There is also a smaller, non-means-tested grant, currently £250, for children whose parents are serving in the armed forces, to "address the emotional and social well-being of these pupils".

How does it work?

Although the government grant to local authorities can only be used for the Pupil Premium, the amount paid out to schools is not ring-fenced. This gives schools the freedom to spend it how they wish. Unfortunately, because other central government grants to schools have been discontinued, some schools have found that the amount paid in Pupil Premium does not fully compensate for what has been lost from the budget. This leads to some hard choices about how to use the money.

The DfE has published a number of suggestions for using the premium. These include:

- One-to-one tuition, based on a range of reading partnerships, not always led by teachers. However, the evidence suggests that it works better when teachers are involved, although the results even without them are generally positive.
- Peer-to-peer tuition. This is aimed at improving the skills and attitudes of both partners. There is some evidence that this works.
- Parental involvement. As in most aspects of children's learning this

has positive outcomes, especially if the parents of disadvantaged children are given help and support.

The DfE guidance includes a provision map, which is a useful chart that shows the factors that influence the success of Pupil Premium interventions. It covers familiar topics such as identification, tracking, monitoring, tailored provision, professional development, and parental involvement.

The DfE has promised further guidance on using the grant.

The governors' role

To get the best out of the scheme, governors should begin by checking that the school is getting all the premium payments to which it is entitled. There should be effective strategies for making sure that all the parents and carers likely to be eligible for FSM and the other two categories are known to the school and the local authority. Some parents can be reluctant to apply for FSM, so most schools will try to make sure that there is no stigma attached to registering. It helps if the school makes parents aware that they are helping the school's budget by claiming their entitlement, such as through information to new parents and reminders in the school newsletter.

Although the grant is not ring-fenced, the government insists that schools will be held to account for how they spend the money. From September 2012, how the premium has been used has been included in the performance tables, and schools are required to publish details on their websites. An amendment to the School Information Regulations specifies that this must include the amount allocated by the Pupil Premium, how it is planned to spend it, how last year's allocation was spent, and what effect on attainment it had on those pupils for whose benefit it is intended. Also, Ofsted inspectors are bound to ask some searching questions about the use of the premium.

The government claims that this will "ensure that parents and others are made fully aware of the attainment of pupils covered by the Premium", though this may over-estimate the extent to which parents access this kind of data. Nevertheless, governors need to make sure that they know how the money has been used, and what success has been achieved with it. The governing body could ask for an annual statement to be made in the autumn term, perhaps as part of the review of public exam results. This should include hard evidence of how the premium has been targeted towards children from low-income families, and whether this has worked.

For further information see *Pupil Premium: What you need to know*, www.education.gov.uk /schools/pupilsupport/premium, and The School Information (England) (Amendment) Regulations 2012, www.legislation.gov.uk/uksi/2012/1124/made.

FELICITY TAYLOR

Policies: A cut too far?

Despite the publication of a list of statutory policies on the DfE website, what policies schools must have is still shrouded in uncertainty.

With the government's aim of reducing bureaucracy we have seen a reduction in the number of policies and documents that governing bodies have to agree. The latest casualties are the requirement to produce a curriculum policy and a written prospectus (see pages 42 and 44). But with these, as with other documents, schools should debate the pros and cons of these freedoms and consider how to continue to discharge their responsibilities for accounting to parents and carers.

A list of statutory policies was not included in the May 2012 update of *The Governors' Guide to the Law*, and instead governors are referred to the DfE website www.education.gov.uk >Schools>Tools and initiatives> Cutting burdens and bureaucracy>bureaucracy>Statutory policies for schools. This list identifies which policies apply in which types of school – academies, maintained schools, PRUs, etc – and how frequently they should be reviewed. Several that previously had been in the list of statutory policies and documents in the previous *Guide to the Law* are omitted.

However, the list only includes policies determined by primary legislation, but there are others, such as a child protection policy, that are specified in statutory guidance. A footnote has been added to the list.

> "There may be instances where statutory guidance states that policies and procedures should be in place. In cases where governing bodies have an obligation to have regard to this guidance, these policies and procedures should be in place unless it can be demonstrated that there is a good reason not to have them. An example of this is the Government's statutory guidance Safeguarding Children and Safer Recruitment in Education."

Governors should therefore be aware of what their obligations are in relation to statutory guidance documents. The DfE website explains that guidance is produced to tell those charged with a duty how powers and duties that are specified in statutes should be exercised. Where it says there is an obligation to "have regard to" guidance the guidance should be followed unless there is a very a good reason not to. This is the case for most of the guidance. However:

> "Very unusually, there are some forms of guidance which must always be followed and which in themselves impose obligations, such as the Admissions Code. In these cases recipients must follow the guidance – with no exceptions. This distinction will be made clear."

So where should we look to see what we should have in place? What guidance documents are relevant? The DfE offered in February 2012 to produce a second list of policies, but at the time of writing this had not been published.

Omissions

Pending such clarification, there are two omissions from the DfE list that affect the protection of staff and children:

- whistle-blowing
- dealing with allegations against staff.

When a school is seeking to achieve the Schools Financial Value Standard it is expected to have a whistle-blowing policy in place. The equivalent document for academies, the Financial Management and Governance Evaluation, also requires a whistle-blowing policy. This policy is crucial in giving staff an unambiguous message about what to do if they have concerns about a colleague's behaviour.

The guidance document on dealing with allegations against staff concerning abuse published in 2011 is considerably shorter than the practice guidance published in 2009. One significant change is that the current version states that "Details of allegations that are found to be malicious should be removed from personnel records." But a school surely must be able to prove that it had fully investigated the allegation. And if the police were involved wouldn't there still be a record on the Police National Computer? Moreover, when a member of staff is accused of abuse it is an extremely stressful experience for all concerned. The governing body ought to ensure that the school has a clear step-by-step policy/protocol/procedure to ensure that it is handled professionally (see page 54).

What's new?

The DfE's list contains three items that were not on previous lists for governors. One of these is **data protection**. An article on the DfE website, www.education.gov.uk/schools/adminandfinance/schooladmin/ims/data-management/dataprotection/a0064534/data-protection, identifies a number of issues that schools must be aware of when collecting and processing data about learners and other individuals. These include the following eight enforceable principles enshrined in the Data Protection Act 1998.

Data must be:

- fairly and lawfully processed
- processed for limited purposes
- adequate, relevant and not excessive
- accurate
- not kept longer than necessary
- processed in accordance with the data subject's rights
- secure
- not transferred to other countries without adequate protection.

To comply with these principles every school processing personal data must notify under the Act. Failure to notify is a criminal offence. You can find out more about your school's need to notify from the Information Commissioner's website: www.ico.gov.uk/for_organisations/data_protection/notification.aspx

The second addition relates to **equality**. Under the 2010 Equality Act schools have both a general duty and specific duties. The general duty requires that a school must have due regard to the need to:

- eliminate discrimination, harassment, victimisation and any other conduct that is prohibited by the Act
- advance equality of opportunity between persons who share a relevant protected characteristic and persons who do not share it
- foster good relations between persons who share a relevant protected characteristic and persons who do not share it.

Implicit here is that when reviewing plans and policies schools will consider the potential impact on different groups.

The protected characteristics are: age (does not apply to pupils; schools can group them however they believe is appropriate); disability; ethnicity and race; gender; gender reassignment; marriage and civil partnership; pregnancy and maternity; religion and belief; sexual identity and orientation. At least some of these will apply to every individual so the Act covers everyone.

Each school needs to meet the specific public sector equality duty by publishing information annually, by 6 April, showing how they comply with the duty. They were also obliged by 6 April 2012 to publish one or more specific and measurable objectives which they included in the school development plan and should now be pursuing. This activity is to be undertaken again within four years. On 15 May 2012 the Home Secretary announced that the planned review of the general and specific duties is being brought forward to see whether it is operating as intended.

The third addition, **premises management**, is rather mystifying. Apart from noting the need to comply with legislation to ensure the safe management of premises, at the time of writing it is not clear what evidence or information has to be published by schools and academies. For background information see Compliance Monitoring for Council Buildings: www.fedps.org.uk/compliance_monitoring.pdf

Whatever is or isn't on the list it is advisable for schools to maintain a list of their policies and key documents, noting who is the lead member of staff, if/how the governing body is involved (essential for statutory policies and documents), and when they are next due for review

MICHELE ROBBINS

Performance management and capability

New performance management regulations came into effect at the beginning of September. For the first time, they create a through passage from performance management to capability proceedings.

Statistics from the General Teaching Council (abolished by the Coalition government) showed that by 2009 they had received 155 referrals of underperforming teachers, with 64 of those concluding in a competency hearing. Of these, 10 resulted in teachers being struck off and 10 in suspensions. Twenty-three teachers were given conditional registration orders on the grounds they did not appear before a disciplinary hearing again, and six were reprimanded.

Clearly, the number of failing teachers was far too low for Michael Gove. The information presented the Secretary of State with something of an open goal: "Heads and teachers (note: no reference to governors)...want a simpler and faster system to deal with teachers who are struggling. For far too long schools have been trapped in complex red tape. Schools must be given the responsibility to deal with this fairly and quickly."

Teacher appraisal was first introduced to schools in England in 1991, following the Education Act of 1986, very late in the day compared to many other businesses, services and industries. There was no link between appraisal and pay.

Since then there have been changes to the performance management (PM) process but technically speaking the term "appraisal", enshrined in primary legislation, remains in force. In effect, they are one and the same thing.

New performance management regulations came into force in 2001, introducing for the first time the responsibility of governors to appraise the headteacher. In line with changes to the teaching workforce in 2006 via The National Agreement, which introduced PPA time, a new pay structure and a general review of staffing structures, performance management was also overhauled. Revised regulations were enacted on 1 September 2007 and were applied for pay progression purposes from 1 September 2008.

With the advent of the Coalition, the Secretary of State sought a faster way of getting rid of more poor teachers, which he aims to achieve by linking together performance management and capability procedures, two processes which till then had been kept very firmly apart.

A further tightening of the screw was then announced by Ofsted. Addressing the Royal Society of Arts in February 2012, Ofsted chief Sir

Michael Wilshaw suggested that 92 to 93 per cent of teachers are currently allowed to pass through the threshold, despite the fact that Ofsted rates 40 per cent of lessons in state schools as not good enough: "Headteachers and governors should worry about performance management more than they have been doing."

Ofsted decided that from September 2012: "Inspectors will evaluate the robustness of performance management arrangements, and consider whether there is a correlation between the quality of teaching in a school and the salary progression of the school's teachers. We will take the necessary steps to ensure that no individual teacher is identified so that confidential information is not revealed." Accordingly, when inspecting schools it will ask them to provide anonymised information of performance management outcomes, in whatever form it is available. It hopes by so doing to discover whether management and governors are properly using performance management as a tool to drive school improvement.

The regulations

The revised PM and capability regulations and documentation are now with us, replacing the 2006 version, in the form of *Teacher appraisal and capability: A model policy for schools* (DfE May 2012) plus supporting documents (ACAS Code of Practice, a flowchart showing the stages and timescale of capability and the Teachers' Standards). The Model Policy forms Part A of the document.

The regulations do not apply to academies and free schools, though they could choose to adopt them wholly or in part. As always it will take a while before the regulations are enacted in every school, because the timing of implementation depends on what stage any school is at in the PM cycle – though the governors may decide to end the existing cycle early.

According to the DfE, the new regulations are intended to:

- introduce simpler performance management regulations, which set a few basic requirements, remove many restrictions (including the so-called "three hour observation rule"), and leave other decisions to schools
- introduce an optional new model policy for schools that deals with both performance and capability/disciplinary issues
- allow poorly performing teachers to be removed in about a term, a process that now often takes a year or more
- clarify that staff illness need not bring disciplinary processes to a halt
- scrap about 60 pages of unnecessary guidance.

The link between performance management and pay remains in place. Confidentiality is still a general principle underlying the policy, but the model policy says that this should not prevent governors being given details that they need "to quality-assure the operation and effectiveness of the appraisal system."

Appraisal of the headteacher

No substantial changes to the performance management of the head-teacher are envisaged and the requirement for governors to use the services of an external adviser in conducting the review remains in place, as enshrined the original legislation. No new governor training is offered. Some LA Governor Services or HR teams still run such training but it is no longer universal and standardised, and is on the wane. Coupled with the dismantling of the SIP programme, inevitably, governors have had to take more direct responsibility for ensuring the robustness of the performance management process. As long as they ensure that those delegated to appraise the headteacher are well trained and/or pass on their skills and experience to fellow governors, the performance management of head-teachers should be effective and remains a key tool in their monitoring and evaluation toolkit.

Capability

The model policy is largely uncontroversial and governors will welcome it, since it precludes the need to write something from scratch. There are clearly indicated paragraphs in italics where the school can adapt the text to suit their school and circumstances.

The new teeth in the document appear in this paragraph: "If the appraiser is not satisfied with progress, the teacher (or headteacher) will be notified in writing that the appraisal system will no longer apply and that their performance will be managed under the capability procedure, and will be invited to a formal capability meeting."

Part B contains the new Capability Procedure, which applies to all teaching staff, including the headteacher. The intention was to speed up what can be a drawn-out process, especially if the member of staff is signed off with stress or other illness as soon as the matter is raised, as often happens. The capability procedure flowchart proposes a minimum 9 week process, excluding any appeal or other complication. Nevertheless, the procedure gives governors the freedom to increase the minimum notice of each stage if they wish.

Whilst the procedure is admirably clear and user-friendly for all parties, it is uncertain that more than a few cases will be resolved in less time than was previously the case, since few are straightforward. Ensuring his new arrangements bring about the changes he wants may be trickier than Michael Gove anticipates, since it will be up to heads and governors to push them through. The history of teachers' performance management and capability gives few indications that change happens fast or willingly. If they are brave enough to seek to remove poorly performing teachers "in about a term, a process that now often takes a year or more" governors will need to gear themselves up for an increase in appeals panel hearings, grievances and employment tribunals.

DAVID MARRIOTT

More or less, reforms to funding

Reforms to the system of passing funds to schools are not as radical as was expected, but still introduce the biggest change for two decades.

The long-expected assault on school funding in the end was only shot from one barrel. Having initiated in 2010 a thorough review of the whole process by which funding passes down from central government to individual maintained schools, the Secretary of State announced in March 2012 that no changes would be made to the national funding formula during the lifetime of this parliament. However, he did say that changes would be made to the local formulas, starting in the financial year 2013-14. In other words, the allocation of money that comes to schools this April will be according to new rules.

The main drift of the changes are twofold, firstly to make school funding much more pupil-led, and secondly to simplify the system. As is inevitable, simplicity means lack of particularity. There is to be greater constraint on how local authorities (LAs) can direct how funds are allocated, and hence less discrimination between schools. Also inevitably, some schools will feel they have done quite well out of the new system, while others will feel that they have been short-changed.

Allowable factors

Although there were some small alterations made in the consultation period, the allowable factors that can be used in distributing funding are as in Michael Gove's March announcement. In the past most LAs have used a large number of factors but these are now to be limited to ten, of which the last three only affect a small number of schools. They are:

- a basic per-pupil amount, as a single unit for each primary school child and either another single unit for each secondary school child, or different units for Key Stage 3 and Key Stage 4 pupils
- deprivation measures
- looked after children
- low-cost, high-incidence special educational needs
- English as an Additional Language – but only for the first three years after the pupil enters the school system
- a lump sum
- rates
- split sites
- Private Finance Initiative (PFI) contracts

- special flexibility for five LAs split between the London fringe area and outside it so as to reflect the different teacher costs.

Small school funding apparently disappears, but the lump sum is intended to replace it. The government has set a cap of £200,000 on this.

Although it is still permissible to target schools with high levels of deprivation, the means of assessing deprivation are limited to free school meals and the Income Deprivation Affecting Children Index. Other measures, such as Education ACORN, will no longer be allowed.

Cluster funding will disappear, which means that schools will have to find other ways of paying for staff previously employed by clusters, such as Parent Support Advisers, if they are to continue.

There is no minimum threshold for the basic per-pupil amount for this coming year, but the government has stated that it will be examining local authorities' formulas with a view to introducing a threshold in 2014-15. However, the Minimum Funding Guarantee still applies, which means that no school will suffer a budget cut of more than 1.5 percent.

Impact

What does this mean for schools? The short answer is that the impact will be noticeable for just about all. For a start, although the funding here is for maintained schools it will have one important effect on schools considering conversion to academy status. The funding for some central education services will not be passed on to LAs by central government, but instead be allocated on a per-pupil basis to both LAs, for maintained schools, and to academies. This will therefore reduce the "extra" money given to academies by local authorities in the Local Authority Central Spend Equivalent Grant.

Then, the new rules should introduce clarity into what has been a murky place for many governors. Those who have struggled to work out the criteria that determined their school's funding should in future find the task easier.

However, schools that benefited from particular factors, such as allocations for gifted and talented children, swimming, the infant class size funding, or for broadband, will find that these have disappeared. Most such factors will be subsumed into the basic per-pupil amount. This will mean that the money that has hitherto been targeted on specific schools will be averaged out, going to both those with needs and those without. Schools that did well under such factors are likely to find that the money at their disposal has decreased.

Overall it seems that primary schools will be better off than secondary schools, particularly small secondary schools. Very small primary schools will generally do quite well, but small-to-medium-sized primaries will be under pressure. These schools will also find it harder to maintain the infant class size maximum of 30 children. Federation may become more popular.

Details are given in *School Funding Reform: Arrangements for 2013-14* which is on the DfE website, www.education.gov.uk.

HARRIET MANSON

Completing the Schools Financial Value Standard

During the course of this school year the governing bodies of most maintained schools will have to complete their first Schools Financial Value Standard (SFVS) return.

The Schools Financial Value Standard is a self-assessment form for governing bodies that is designed to produce good financial practices, protect schools against fraud, and harness financial decisions to the drive to school improvement. It is less onerous than its predecessor, the Financial Management Standard in Schools, but it still needs completing with care.

The final date for submission to local authorities (LAs) is 31 March 2013, but LAs are generally asking for it earlier, and for many governing bodies completing the form is a job for the autumn term. A few governing bodies, those that did not achieve FMSiS, should already have completed their first SFVS, as these were required by 31 March 2012.

SFVS does not apply to academies, which instead complete a Financial Management and Governance Evaluation in the spring term each year.

Procedure

Responsibility for completing the SFVS rests with the governing body, and it is one of the documents that governing bodies should complete themselves, even if some of the work is delegated to the senior staff. Indeed, several of the questions asked in the form are specifically about governance arrangements. This does not necessarily mean that completion of the form should be handled in a full governing body meeting; if your school has a finance committee, SFVS should be its responsibility and added to that committee's terms of reference.

SFVS consists of 23 factual questions, for each of which you answer "yes", "no" or "in part". For each question there is also a box for "Comments, Evidence and Proposed Actions" where you should determine how the governing body acts on its answers. For "yes" answers the evidence should be given. Stand back from the answer you give and be critical; if the evidence is not convincing then the question needs to be revisited. For "no" or "in part" answers, write in the box what action governors and staff agree will be taken to remedy the deficiency. Whatever is decided must be monitored at future meetings. At the end of the form you are asked for a summary action plan and timetable for actions.

Given the importance of proper control of finance, the governing body, or its finance committee, should always ensure that it is confident that the information given is correct and can be shown to be so.

The governing body should submit the form annually to its local authority. The LA will not validate the form, but is expected to use it in considering its programme of financial assessment of schools, and to gauge its accuracy when it conducts an audit of the school. Any schools which fail to submit the form are likely to be subject to a notice of concern from the LA, and if it has serious and continuing worries the LA may withdraw its financial delegation.

Where to go for more information

The DfE provides support notes for each question on the form. These give detailed information under a standard three headings for each:

- What does the question mean?
- Good practice
- What do you do if things are not right in your school?

The information varies from basic definitions to detailed guidance on practice. As SFVS makes the governing body reflect on such things as its financial competence, whether it receives the monitoring information it needs, whether budgeting links clearly to the school's plans for raising standards, and whether the school has a proper accounting system, in their entirety these notes add up to a comprehensive guide for all finance committees.

They can be found on www.education.gov.uk>Schools>Administration and finance>Schools financial management>Schools Financial Value Standard. The Standard itself can be downloaded from the same part of the site.

STEPHEN ADAMSON

The Ofsted view

From the grade descriptor of "outstanding" leadership and management.

- The pursuit of excellence in all of the school's activities is demonstrated by an uncompromising and highly successful drive to strongly improve, or maintain, the highest levels of achievement and personal development for all pupils over a sustained period of time.
- All leaders and managers, including those responsible for governance, are highly ambitious for the pupils and lead by example. They base their actions on a deep and accurate understanding of the school's performance, and of staff and pupils' skills and attributes.
- Governors, or those with a similar responsibility, robustly hold senior leaders to account for all aspects of the school's performance.
  [...]
- Through highly effective, rigorous planning and controls, governors ensure financial stability, including the effective and efficient management of financial resources such as the Pupil Premium funding. This leads to the excellent deployment of staff and resources to the benefit of all groups of pupils.

Ofsted inspection framework September 2012

Governor responsibilities on pupil behaviour

Governors of both maintained schools and academies have responsibility for pupil behaviour, but they do not draw up the behaviour policy. Their role is agree principles with the headteacher or principal which form its basis.

In 2012 the DfE published *Ensuring Good Behaviour in Schools: A summary for head teachers, governing bodies, teachers, parents and pupils*, which states: "Every school must have a behaviour policy. The governing body is responsible for setting general principles that inform the behaviour policy. The governing body must consult the head teacher, school staff, parents and pupils when developing these principles. Head teachers are responsible for developing the behaviour policy in the context of this framework."

This restatement of requirements first established in the Education and Inspections Act 2006 seems clear enough. What, though, are we supposed to put into that principles document? There is no "official" guidance on this and there's no point waiting for it since the DfE are on a mission to reduce the bureaucratic burden on schools and governors, which includes detailed guidance and advice.

The website Teaching Expertise (www.teachingexpertise.com) offers the following help:

"Principles that most assist the headteacher:

- are based on the school's values
- can be explained to pupils of any age or ability
- represent widespread agreement about standards amongst pupils, staff (including union representatives) and parents
- encourage a healthy balance between rewards and sanctions to encourage positive behaviour
- promote behaviour improvement as a means of improving learning and teaching
- are challenging but realistic and appropriate for development as the school builds on its successes".

The web is also a rich source of sample school behaviour policies, though not all contain the required principles and are not quality-assured, so must be treated with caution.

Ofsted inspect behaviour and attendance as one of the four key areas of school performance. The 2012 Framework says: "When evaluating the quality of leadership and management at all levels, including, where relevant, governors, inspectors consider whether they improve teaching and learning, including the management of pupils' behaviour"

This clearly emphasises the need for governors' principles to reflect a focus on positive behaviour management, social and emotional learning and the promotion of behaviours for learning rather than just discipline (as in bullet point 5 above) – and implies that one key way of evaluating the efficacy of the behaviour policy is through its impact on the effectiveness of learning.

Broad and ambitious principles

In drawing up their principles governors might also reflect on the 10 principles of effective behaviour management identified by Sir Alan Steer in *Learning Behaviour Principles and Practice – What works in schools* (Section 2 of the report of the Practitioners' on School Behaviour and Discipline chaired by Alan Steer) published by the DfES in 2006:

1. consistency of approach by all school staff
2. effective school leadership ("Head teachers and governors have a critical role in identifying and developing values and expectations that are shared by pupils, parents and staff")
3. good classroom management, learning and teaching
4. a range of clear, appropriate rewards and sanctions
5. behaviour strategies and the teaching of good behaviour
6. staff development and support
7. pupil support systems
8. liaison with parents and other agencies
9. effective arrangements for managing pupil transition
10. organising the school day and its facilities to take account of behaviour issues.

Whatever principles we draw up should enable the above to work well. An effective whole school behaviour policy is exactly that: it affects and relates to every aspect of school policy and practice, so our principles must be equally broad and ambitious.

If governors are still unsure what a set of principles might look like, there are some good examples on the web, such as those for Cannock Chase High School and Queen's Inclosure Primary School in Waterlooville.

Finally, how would we know if our principles were being enacted fully? These are Ofsted's descriptors of outstanding behaviour:

- Parents, carers, staff and pupils are highly positive about behaviour and safety.
- Pupils make an exceptional contribution to a safe, positive learning environment. They make every effort to ensure that others learn and thrive in an atmosphere of respect and dignity.
- Pupils show very high levels of engagement, courtesy, collaboration and cooperation in and out of lessons. They have excellent, enthusi-

astic attitudes to learning, enabling lessons to proceed without interruption.

- Pupils are consistently punctual in arriving at school and lessons. They are highly adept at managing their own behaviour in the classroom and in social situations, supported by systematic, consistently applied approaches to behaviour management. They are very calm, orderly and considerate when moving around the school.
- There are excellent improvements in behaviour over time for any individuals or groups with particular behavioural difficulties.
- Instances of bullying, including for example, cyber-bullying and prejudice-based bullying related to special educational need, sexual orientation, sex, race, religion and belief, gender reassignment or disability, are extremely rare.
- Pupils are acutely aware of different forms of bullying and actively try to prevent it from occurring.
- The school has an active and highly effective approach to identifying and tackling bullying.
- All groups of pupils feel safe at school at all times. They understand very clearly what constitutes unsafe situations and are highly aware of how to keep themselves and others safe.
- It is likely that attendance will be above average for all groups of pupils or will show sustained and convincing improvement over time.

DAVID MARRIOTT

The Ofsted view

"My answer is that we want them [school governors] to govern. In essence, what does this mean?

It means that we want you to work with the leaders of your schools to be both strategic and pragmatic in delivering good outcomes for all your children and young people. Not satisfactory, but good.

We want you to strengthen your schools' professional leadership by appointing the right people to the right jobs.

And we want you to hold them to account for the progress and outcomes they achieve in your schools.

It sounds simple, but you know how hard that can be. But without strong and effective governance, our schools simply won't be as good as they can be.

Your role is fundamental and you should never forget that."

Sir Michael Wilshaw, HMCI, to the NGA Policy Conference, June 2012

Governing the curriculum

With greater emphasis on their responsibility for school standards, governors need to understand just what their role in the curriculum is.

Longer-serving governors will realise that the school's curriculum is reviewed and revised regularly. To a large extent this depends on central government's thinking in terms of the National Curriculum, but research evidence on how children learn, and how this might improve their life chances, should also have an impact. Governors must ensure that the school complies with legislation and any regulations or statutory guidance.

The governing body gives strategic direction to the school with a view to raising standards of achievement. Tests and examinations are based on the subjects that must be delivered, so governing bodies should be aware of what has to be provided statutorily and hold the school's leaders to account for its level of success. This means discussing the curriculum regularly, so that governors know what pupils are studying, and why, and can monitor the progress they make.

However, the governing body has responsibility for the whole curriculum offered by the school, and this is where it can ensure the breadth and balance to their learning that children and young people need so as to be able to make informed decisions about their own futures. Governors should work with the school's leaders to consider the school in its community and wider context, and judge for themselves what wider learning opportunities the pupils will benefit from.

Knowing *what* is provided is only part of the task. Governing bodies must also ensure that the whole curriculum is delivered in such a way that it enables pupils at all levels of ability to achieve their potential, and also realises the school's overall objectives.

It is also important to understand what Ofsted expects of the governing body in fulfilling its curriculum responsibilities. The 2012 Evaluation Schedule says little about actual curriculum content, but the sections on achievement, quality of teaching and leadership and management each make oblique reference to what is expected.

Doing this effectively

Firstly, governors should remember that theirs is a strategic role, and ensure that they do not impinge on the headteacher's/principle's operational role. The governing body may be ultimately responsible in broad terms for what is taught in the school, but the headteacher puts it into action.

Contrary to some popular thinking, governing bodies do not have to approve subject policies, and certainly not schemes of work. These are the professionals' working documents; they do not need formal adoption by governors.

Most governing bodies have a committee structure, with one committee covering curriculum content and school standards. This committee should ask questions about:

- statutory requirements, and whether the school meets these, both in terms of content and the amount of teaching time for each subject
- details of the different work provided for the varying levels of ability in the school, from the gifted children to those with special needs, and how this is delivered, to ensure that children are appropriately supported
- the resources needed to meet the needs of the whole curriculum, and the sustainability of the non-statutory elements (and making recommendations to a Finance Committee)
- changes planned for the curriculum and how the school will meet those and others imposed externally, i.e. from central government
- through the headteacher, the overall quality of teaching, and strategies for improvement where necessary
- review of policies that affect the curriculum: sex and relationships education, SEN, gifted and talented, RE, collective worship
- annual assessment and examination arrangements, to comply with national requirements
- what the school is saying in its self-evaluation document.

This committee may also review results data, noting particularly:

- the level of progress pupils make, and how this will be maintained or improved
- comparisons between teachers' predictions and actual results of both external and internal tests, to see where variances exist and the reasons for them.

Governors should try to see the school's curriculum in action. This could be by individuals attached to subject areas as "linked governors", or by the committee making group visits to the school to see a planned improvement or development in operation.

Governing bodies are no longer required to have a curriculum policy (since September 2012), but parents must be told about the curriculum offered. The governing body is responsible for ensuring this information is available, either online or in another format.

The Governor's Guide to the Law contains much information about the governing body's responsibilities for the curriculum. Although governing bodies of academies and Free Schools do not have to follow the National Curriculum, they still have overall responsibility for the curriculum and may find the Guide useful (see page 84).

SUE PLATT

Bringing computing back into schools

The government has responded to recent claims that ICT in schools only teaches how to be a computer user, and has indicated a major overhaul of this important part of the compulsory curriculum.

Following a speech by the Secretary of State for Education at the BETT Show in January 2012, it is clear that successful schools will be expected in future to teach a deeper and broader understanding of ICT, one that includes computer science as well as information technology. Computer science is a discipline, like maths or physics, whose principles and techniques underpin the digital world in which we now live. While ICT focuses on teaching pupils how to *use* software, typically packages like Microsoft Excel and PowerPoint, computer science involves *writing* computer software – which is the core skill behind many of the world's leading computer companies such as Facebook, Google and Microsoft.

Immediately following BETT, the Royal Society published their report *Shut Down or Restart: The way forward for computing in UK schools.* This is an authoritative, evidence-based study that explains the importance of computer science, information technology and digital literacy.

In his speech at BETT the Secretary of State also explained his hope that eventually computer science will be considered for inclusion in the EBac, both because of its educational value as a rigorous academic subject in its own right and also because of its economic importance to the UK.

Establishing computer science in our curriculum, from primary school onwards, represents both a strategic opportunity and a challenge for governors and school leaders. It is an opportunity because we have ample evidence of how creative, inspirational, and plain useful computer science is at school. Whereas many pupils today find ICT dull, the evidence from schools which have introduced computer science is that pupils, particularly the more able, enjoy it far more – both the intellectual challenge and the chance to build real computer programs.

It is a challenge because nationally we are starting from a very low base, and our teachers are often willing but under-qualified. Hundreds of schools are rising to this challenge, and are now implementing the switch to computer science. There is plenty of support available, particularly the Computing at School strategic information pack (www.bcs.org/csteachingexcellence), which is specifically addressed to school leaders.

You may want to consider:

- Are all our pupils engaged in ICT, as it is taught in our school at the moment?

- Are our ICT teachers equipped to teach computer science, and how can we support them in taking appropriate CPD?
- (For secondary schools) Are we offering computer science GCSE and A Level and if not, why not?

There is also plenty of help for schools that want to do more. The representative body for computing in schools is Computing at School (CAS) – www.computingatschool.org.uk. CAS offers teachers and governors help and support in promoting computing via local "hubs" of schools. CAS is also working with the British Computing Society to establish a Network of Teaching Excellence in Computer Science. As part of the Network, and in partnership with universities, CAS is launching a national programme of CPD to equip teachers with subject knowledge to support computer science. If your school has decided to teach computer science at any level, you should be encouraging it to join this network.

NEIL COLLINS AND SIMON PEYTON-JONES

What schools have to publish

Schools no longer have to publish a printed prospectus. Instead their websites must either contain information on the following or direct parents to where they can find it:

- SATS or GCSE results -- with percentages of pupils attaining level 4 and level 5 in English and maths at Key Stage 2 and of those attaining five A*-C GCSEs in English and maths and achieving the English Baccalaureate at Key Stage 4, plus in both Key Stages the percentages making the expected degree of progress
- where school performance tables can be accessed
- the school's admission arrangements
- the school's ethos and values
- the most recent Ofsted report
- the school's charging and behaviour policies,
- information on the school's curriculum for each academic year, GCSE courses at Key Stage 4 plus other courses offered and the qualifications they can lead to; phonics or reading schemes used at Key Stage 1, and details of how the school meets the needs of children with SEN.

The school's name, address, phone number and a contact name must also be given.

Schools must also publish on their websites information on how they spend the Pupil Premium. This must include the amount of Pupil Premium the school has received for the current academic year, details of how it is intended that the allocation will be spent, details of how the previous academic year's allocation was spent, and the effect of this expenditure on the educational attainment of those pupils at the school in respect of whom the Pupil Premium was allocated.

The school must provide parents with a paper copy of any of the above information, if requested, free of charge.

See The School Information (England) (Amended) Regulations 2012.

New tunes for Wales

In a drive to improve schools, the Welsh Government is making some radical changes, including taking an important step towards mandatory training for governors.

The school year 2011-12 in Wales was a year of relentless focus on implementation of the school improvement agenda set out in the "Twenty Points" speech by the Education Minister, Leighton Andrews, in February 2011. It was also a year in which the contribution governors can make to school improvement was in the spotlight.

The Minister's 20-point programme for school improvement was stimulated by the disappointing results for Welsh 15-year-olds in the 2009 Programme for International Student Assessment (PISA). His ideas have now been fleshed out, and there are three key aspects.

New statutory powers

The School Standards and Organisation Bill (Wales) has been published. This is the first Education Bill to come before the Assembly under its new powers to enact primary legislation.

School improvement is at the heart of the Bill, which will consolidate, rationalise and reform the current law on intervention by local authorities in schools that are causing concern. It will also sharpen the powers of the Minister to intervene directly in schools where local authorities fail to act, and to intervene in local authorities themselves.

In addition, the Minister will have powers to issue statutory school improvement guidance to local authorities, governing bodies and headteachers. The guidance will set out the best practice currently available, and schools will have a statutory duty to follow it. The Minister will be able to enforce this through a statutory power of direction.

Schools that require intervention will be identified through a banding system that measures comparative performance, mainly in aspects of pupil attainment, but also taking into account pupil attendance. Secondary school bandings are already in place, but the introduction of primary school banding has been postponed until September 2014 because the Minister is not satisfied that pupil attainment measured solely by teacher assessment is rigorous enough. In September 2014 the results of new statutory literacy and numeracy tests will be available, and these will be the determining factor in primary school bandings.

National literacy and numeracy plans

These tests result from Leighton Andrews' belief that "getting literacy and numeracy right is the key to boosting performance" and that this cannot be left to the discretion of individual schools or local authorities. During

2013 national literacy and numeracy plans are to be introduced within a statutory framework, with both primary and secondary schools being expected to ensure that literacy and numeracy teaching is embedded in all subjects. The national tests will apply to all pupils from Year 2 to Year 9. Schools will be expected to monitor individual pupil progress against annual targets and to report annually to parents.

The Minister is concerned not just to boost literacy and numeracy standards overall, but to reduce the impact of poverty on standards. To this end, and – unusually for him – following England's lead, a pupil deprivation grant has been introduced. Schools now receive £450 per annum for each pupil on the free school meals register. However, to secure this extra funding, schools have to present a detailed plan to their local authority on how the money will be used to raise the standards attained by such pupils.

Mandatory governor training

The Minister sees governors as being key drivers for school improvement, but they need to have the appropriate skills and knowledge. Statutory powers are already in place for compulsory training for new governors and chairs of governors, and detailed proposals have now emerged from the Welsh Government. New governors will have to complete induction training within 12 months of their election or appointment, while newly elected chairs of governors will have to complete chair's training within six months. Governors who rejoin a governing body after a break in service of five years will be required to do the induction training, and there will be a similar provision for those re-elected as chair after a five-year break. There will also be a requirement on new governors to undertake school performance data training within a 12-month period. This is regarded as a critical aspect of the governors' monitoring role.

Of course, the implication for those who do not complete the training within the prescribed period is that they will be disqualified from office.

The scope and content of the mandatory training of governors has been drawn up with the involvement of all interested parties, including Governors Wales. It means a significant change to the concept of the "volunteer" governor, but recognises of the importance of governors in securing school improvement. At this stage, it is unclear what funding will be available to meet the cost of all this extra training.

Reaction

While there is general support in Welsh education circles, including governors, for Leighton Andrews' measures to improve schools, there is some concern about the centralisation of education policy that they entail. However, judgement is likely to be reserved until the impact of the programme becomes clear.

ALLAN TAIT

Appointing headteachers

As the high number of re-advertisements witnesses, there is still a shortage of headteachers. It's wise to think ahead before the resignation letter arrives.

Governors are often tempted to rush into finding a quick replacement when their headteacher/principal resigns. This can sometimes produce a narrow field and lead to expensive mistakes. However, you can buy yourself more time by considering possible temporary leadership solutions. There may be staff in the school who would benefit from being an acting head, with support from a head in a neighbouring school, or a deputy head from another school, released from it to give them practical experience of headship elsewhere, or a head who can take on the acting headship of another school while continuing in their own.

Thinking ahead

A wise governing body will think ahead so that learning of the headteacher's resignation or retirement does not cause panic. This is a matter of being strategic. Develop the leadership potential of your staff. While they are honing their leadership skills they will contribute more to your school, and also your school will establish a reputation which will make it much easier to recruit bright and ambitious staff, including a headteacher.

Work collaboratively with other schools. Staff will develop skills and understanding that benefit pupils and develop leadership capacity. This is particularly important in small schools. Where collaboration is already working well, it becomes easier to negotiate temporary arrangements for seconding acting heads.

Don't be afraid to discuss the possibility of federation or joining a multi-academy trust where close collaboration is formalised under a single governing body or board of directors (see pages 16–17). You may restructure to have an executive head over two or more schools or academies, and advertise a "head of school" post to fill an individual school vacancy. Some leaders are attracted to those posts because they welcome the opportunity to be members of a larger leadership team.

The recruitment process

There are several steps to the actual recruitment.

The full governing body must establish a panel of governors to carry out the process and make a recommendation on the actual appointment back to it at the end of the process. Aim to have the full range of perspectives in the group to ensure that recommendations will be trusted by all governing body members. Don't automatically exclude staff governors – but avoid choosing any staff governor who stands to gain directly from the decision. Your current head must play no part in the appointment of a successor. At least one member of the panel must have completed the accredited Safer Recruitment course.

Ensure that the full governing body agrees the seven-point Individual School Range (ISR), which determines the head's pay scale. This information needs to be included in your advert. The rules for determining the ISR are set out in the *School Teachers' Pay and Conditions Document* but there is some discretion: consider whether you might need to pay more than to the previous incumbent in order to attract a suitable applicant.

Exploit the benefits of using an outside expert adviser. This may be a representative of the LA (and diocese in church schools) or trust, or you may buy a consultancy from a local head. External experts can, however, only advise; the decision on the appointment is made by governors.

Think carefully about how to describe the challenges and opportunities that the job presents. You will want to make the job look attractive, but don't misrepresent any problems. Convey a welcoming message to encourage applications, while making clear what the school's safeguarding arrangements are, to deter undesirable applicants.

Think carefully about your selection criteria. These are usually divided into "essential" and "desirable". Be careful not to put so much in the essential column that you can't appoint someone who would otherwise be an excellent match. (Something is essential if it can't be obtained in a few months through training and the consequences of your head not having it from day one would be catastrophic.)

Give yourselves sufficient time to make robust decisions at the shortlisting stage. Ensure all members of the panel evaluate each application against the agreed selection criteria. When the panel meets those individual evaluations will be the basis for discussion about which candidates to shortlist. Applicants are entitled to be told why they have not been shortlisted; the reasons you give must relate directly to the selection criteria.

Ensure you have sufficient time to receive references before interviews. It is advisable to send referees a questionnaire rather than allowing referees to make general – perhaps coded – comments. Although some people leave checking references until after the interviews, it is sensible to read references in advance in case there is anything in them that you would want to clarify with a candidate.

Structure interview tasks and questions to enable governors to judge key aspects of your selection criteria. Consider how to judge candidates' rapport with pupils and staff. A presentation exercise can test candidates' clarity of thought and ability to persuade. Interview questions should be open-ended and ask for responses based on actual experience (rather than hypothetical situations). Don't be afraid to ask follow-up questions based on what each candidate says; "equal opportunities" does not mean rigidly identical questions.

Detailed advice is usually available from LAs, which will generally also support academies if asked.

MARTIN POUNCE

Support for Chairs from the National College

The National College's role has been enhanced, to include training chairs of governors. The first fruits of this are now available.

In *The Importance of Teaching* White Paper, Michael Gove announced an extension to the National College's brief to include governance, for the first time. Throughout 2011 the College worked with national governance organisations and others to develop a new national training programme for chairs, a small army of National Leaders of Governance (NLGs) and free resources for governors in general. In a later development in April 2012, the College became one of four executive agencies of the DfE, ending its independence. Employees became civil servants, there to do the bidding of the Department and its Secretary of State.

The Chairs of Governors Development Programme

During the spring and summer of 2012 a development programme for chairs was road-tested and an invitation was offered to tender for licences to deliver it from the autumn onwards. According to College publicity, "The programme gives chairs the opportunity to develop their leadership skills through facilitated workshops, online activities, personal reflection and school-based learning. Individual units can be studied consecutively or you can choose to undertake a single unit dependent on your needs."

Candidates may work through any or all of the three units:

- The role of the chair, the leader
- Leading the governing body and effective governance
- Leading change and continuous improvement.

Each unit includes a workshop that provides opportunities to collaborate and learn with peers, opportunities to reflect on leadership practice, and school-based activities designed to lead to school improvement. Each student is given access to a mentor for support, guidance and challenge, has access to interactive online materials, and is guided by an online leadership diagnostic.

However, there are several barriers to widespread take-up. An obvious one is cost. Any organisation (or "partnership" as they are known) that wins a licence to deliver the training may charge what they like for the course, though £350 has been given as a guide figure. They may be some financial support from the National College for a small number of candidates. Another is time. Because the College was obliged to ensure parity between this training and comparable opportunities for heads and other education professionals, the bar was set high. An aspect of this expectation is that each unit is meant to take 50 hours, though this can include time spent in meetings, for example. A further problem could be geography, since the face-to-face session may not be offered very locally and governors are notoriously averse to travelling very far for their training.

Despite these practical issues, the programme is to be welcomed and much will be learned from its implementation.

National Leaders of Governance (NLGs)

There is no doubt that chairs of governors, especially those new to the role, can benefit enormously from the support of a more experienced and skilful mentor. Alongside the development programme the College has recruited two cohorts of NLGs, whose job is essentially to mentor chairs of governors needing support – because they are new and in a struggling school, Ofsted has put the school in a category, working practices need developing, or for a variety of other reasons.

Provided they meet a demanding set of eligibility criteria, NLGs undergo a rigorous selection and training process, including practical assessment of their interpersonal skills, which are paramount.

There is a slight danger that NLGs could turn out to be a solution in search of a problem, since traditionally chairs have been supported as individuals by local governor support teams, some of whom also offer formal or informal mentoring. Nonetheless, funding cuts are limiting those teams' capacity to continue such support, so it may be that the NLGs' time has come. If so, this new national resource will be seen to have been a timely and helpful development.

There remains a practical issue about just how an individual chair's mentoring needs will come to light, be picked up and an appropriate NLG assigned to the case. Once again, local governor services (or other LA officers) could be invaluable in identifying need and seeking NLG support. It is encouraging that National College employees have been assiduous in recognising the need to work in partnership with governance organisations and specialists.

Free resources for governors

The College website, which is now part of the DfE's website (www.education.gov.uk/nationalcollege), offers what will be an expanding library of useful resources for chairs and governors in general, including the booklet developed in conjunction with the National Governors' Association, *Leading Governors*. Membership is free to any governor.

These developments are to be welcomed and should complement any services for governors offered locally. It will be interesting to see how successful they are since any extension of the College's remit to provide more general training and support for all governors may well depend on it.

DAVID MARRIOTT

New rules on exclusion

New guidance on exclusions contains one major change to the procedure and several smaller ones that governors need to note.

The DfE has published new guidance on exclusions, *Exclusion from Maintained Schools, Academies and Pupil Referral Units in England – A guide for those with legal responsibilities in relation to exclusion.* Having come into effect on 1 September 2012, it takes account of new regulations on school behaviour published this year, and contains guidelines to which people must have regard when carrying out their functions in relation to exclusions. The DfE emphasises that "have regard to" doesn't mean that people must follow every detail, but that the guidance should be followed unless there is good reason not to. The guidance, which, as the title says, applies equally to academies and maintained schools, is on the DfE website, under Schools>Leadership and governance>Statutory guidance for schools.

Appeals

The biggest change from previous guidance on the subject is not in how governing bodies should handle exclusions hearings but in what can come later. If a parent is unhappy with a decision to uphold an exclusion they can appeal to an independent review panel. This replaces the independent appeal panel, and the change of wording is significant. The new panel does not have the power to overturn a decision to exclude, but only to direct a governing body to reconsider a decision. It can do this if it considers that the school has acted in an unlawful or irrational manner, or if decides that the exclusions process has been flawed. The panel has to be set up by the local authority for maintained schools and the academy trust for academies.

If the independent review panel directs reconsideration, the governing body or its panel has to meet within ten days. It can stand by its original decision and not reinstate the pupil, but if so the school will be required to pay £4000 towards the cost of alternative provision. In the case of maintained schools the money will be deducted from the school's budget; academies must pay the sum over the local authority.

Exclusion procedure

The new guidance is shorter than its predecessor, with most of the good practice guidance stripped out. It reiterates that the governing body should meet within 15 days to review a headteacher's decision to exclude when:

- the exclusion is permanent
- it is a fixed period exclusion which would bring the pupil's total number of school days of exclusion to more than 15 in a term; or

- it would result in a pupil missing a public examination or national curriculum test.

It states that a child should only be excluded permanently if

- in response to serious or persistent breaches of the school's behaviour policy; and
- where allowing the pupil to remain in school would seriously harm the education or welfare of the pupil or others in the school.

The word "persistent" should be noted as previous guidance only gave "serious breaches" as the grounds for permanent exclusion.

Certain groups of children are subject to much higher exclusion rates than the average, particularly those with special educational needs, looked after children, children in receipt of free school meals, and some ethnic groups. The guidance urges schools to ensure that their policies and practices do not discriminate against these children. Headteachers should particularly try to avoid permanently excluding looked after children or those with statements of special education need as these children suffer most from the effects of exclusion. Governors reviewing permanent exclusions should ask about the support that has been offered to any such children that come before them, and what alternatives to exclusion have been explored.

Guidance is provided for governors hearing exclusions on how the panel should be conducted. This includes the need for confidentiality and to circulate written evidence to the panel, parents and person representing the school before the hearing, normally five school days in advance. They should also take steps to encourage the pupil to attend, as well as his/her parent or carer, and to speak, or for the pupil to feed in their views if they decide not to attend. Hearings of permanent exclusions should be arranged within 15 days of the exclusion being made, as previously.

Although the guidance only differs from its predecessor in a few key points, these are significant enough for governors experienced in sitting on exclusion panels to need to consult it to ensure that they are up to date.

STEPHEN ADAMSON

The Ofsted view

"Most commonly, the governing body knew too little about the school because monitoring was not rigorous or because over-generous self review judgements were accepted without sufficient challenge: at times of change and in an inherently challenging sector, they accepted too much on trust."

Ofsted Annual Report 2010/11

Learning the lessons about safeguarding children

Two recent publications have highlighted the need for constant vigilance if we are to safeguard children and promote their welfare.

North Somerset's Safeguarding Children's Board (NSSCB) *Serious Case Review of Nigel Leat* (www.northsomersetlscb.org.uk/uploads/files/282.pdf) and the first research report by the Independent Safeguarding Authority, *Safeguarding in the Workplace: What are the lessons to be learned from cases referred to the Independent Safeguarding Authority?*, (www.isa.homeoffice.gov.uk/pdf/ISA%20Research%20Report%20Ver%203-11.pdf) both raise important safeguarding issues for schools.

Nigel Leat Serious Case Review (SCR)

In June 2011 Nigel Leat, a teacher at a First school in Somerset, was jailed indefinitely having pleaded guilty to abusing children in his school for 14 years. Concerns had been raised by his colleagues over 30 incidents, and one teacher had included worries in an end-of-year report to governors. The serious case review found that: "There was an endemic culture of neglect" and "a significant failure to comply with any of the principles of any of the guidance designed to promote safer working practice within schools". It also found that "There is no evidence that at any other time in his life or in any activity out of work he might pose a risk to children", so his CRB check would have given no cause for concern. It also noted: "The chair of governors felt that the relationship between governors and the school was generally good but they found some difficulty when they challenged the school or requested further information."

The report concluded that all school governing bodies in North Somerset should be alerted to the need to "rigorously and intrusively" ensure that their schools' safeguarding policies and practices are effective.

Many local authorities provide frameworks to underpin safeguarding audits, but if completing them is a tick-box activity they are of little value. For example, noting that all staff have received safeguarding training does not guarantee that they are acting on it and that it is helping to keep children safe. When making judgements about the school's performance across all aspects of its work governors need to seek evidence of impact.

The 2009 Ofsted Evaluation schedule provides a detailed description of what comes under the umbrella of safeguarding. It also provides descriptors for outstanding, good, satisfactory and inadequate practice. Together they give all of us in schools a clear steer about relevant policies, documents and procedures.

Taking a strategic approach, the governing body should agree with staff a statement about the school's principles for safeguarding children, which it could follow with a list of the relevant policies and documents. There will be several of these, including Child Protection, E-safety, Health and Safety, Providing First Aid, and Use of Physical Intervention. For guidance on monitoring and evaluating policies, see page 30.

The lessons drawn by the SCR Team included:

- It is essential for schools to keep accurate records of all incidents and concerns arising in connection with members of staff in order that historical patterns can be detected.
- While it is important to protect staff against malicious allegations, all concerns and complaints need to be treated in an open minded way and all evidence carefully recorded.
- The teacher's behaviour conformed to typical grooming for sexual abuse. This was not recognised by staff. Child protection training for school staff should aim to help the recognition of such behaviour, and ensure that external advice is sought in any case causing concern.

The Independent Safeguarding Authority (ISA) report

The ISA's report is based on a selection of 100 referrals relating to abuse of children. Of these, 58 percent were sexual, 27 percent physical, 9 percent emotional, and 6 percent neglect; 24 involved teachers and 14 support staff.

The ISA concluded that all staff and volunteers need to be subject to robust recruitment and selection procedures and to be made fully aware of their responsibility to safeguard children and promote their welfare. In over half the cases multiple behaviour types were evidenced. For example, physical abuse was often preceded by verbal or emotional abuse in the form of threats. In cases of sexual abuse, grooming behaviour amounted to emotional manipulation. In just over three quarters of the cases there were repeated or multiple instances of allegedly harmful or abusive behaviour. The report points out that viewed in isolation they might not result in action being taken.

Warning signs of abuse included:

- engaging in unnecessary or inappropriate physical contact with children
- excessive or unnecessary social communication with children outside the work setting
- poor general performance as a teacher
- poor attendance or high levels of sick leave
- previous criminal convictions.

The report says that employers must set acceptable standards of conduct and ensure that these are communicated to all new staff during their induction, not just to new recruits to the profession. They must create an open culture where everyone knows how to raise a concern and can be confident that it will be dealt with professionally. There should be systems for recording instances of poor conduct to identify any patterns that emerge and to minimise the risk of poor behaviour escalating into abuse. (This and the previous point echo the findings of the SCR.)

The report also advocates CRB checks being completed before an individual starts work, and then repeating checks. This is contrary to the advice given to inspectors by Ofsted in its publication *Inspecting Safeguarding, Briefing for section 5 inspection*, which states that "new members of staff can take up their posts prior to a full CRB check as long as they work under close supervision of a colleague who has such clearance" and that "no further checks are required for any staff unless the person has a break in service of more than three months".

The lessons of the report are:

- When employing staff through agencies checks should be made as to the completion of appropriate safeguarding training.
- All staff should receive regular refresher safeguarding training, including guidance on the use of social media.

This section of the ISA report concludes with two recommendations about early and appropriate involvement of the Local Authority Designated Officer and statutory intervention teams when abuse is suspected, echoing another of the findings of the SCR team.

In conclusion

Governing bodies, leadership teams and staff are challenged to raise standards and narrow gaps. In doing so we must not lose sight of the equally important responsibilities to safeguard children and promote their welfare. All governors cannot do everything. Distribution of responsibilities around committees and individual governors is as important as staff assuming key roles and responsibilities. The designated governor for safeguarding could work with relevant members of staff to ensure that the evidence base in the audit is robust. An annual report to the governing body could summarise findings.

MICHELE ROBBINS

The Ofsted view

On schools to be judged "with serious weaknessess" rather than "requiring special measures": "These are schools where there are serious concerns about aspects of the quality of education and where one or more of the key areas of achievement, the quality of teaching and behaviour and safety are judged inadequate (grade 4). These schools do not require special measures, as the school leaders and governors are demonstrating their capacity to improve these schools."

FAQs on responses to Ofsted's consultation 'A good education for all'

The governors' national association

The National Governors' Association, the representative body for school governors in England, plays a substantial part in supporting governance.

Governors in England have a single body that represents them nationally, the National Governors' Association. Formed in 2006 by the merger of the National Association of School Governors and the National Governors' Council, the NGA has roots that can be traced back over 40 years. Since the early days after the merger the size and influence of the NGA have increased considerably.

The NGA's operations can be grouped under three headings:

- communication and support
- representation
- advancement of governance.

Communication and support

NGA keeps its members up to date with the rapid succession of change in the educational world by publishing a weekly e-newsletter, which digests those elements of the week's news that are relevant to school governors. A broader perspective on what is going on is provided in its bi-monthly magazine, *Governing Matters*, which also includes articles from the DfE and other organisations with important messages for governors.

The NGA's website (www.nga.org.uk) holds a range of different types of support for governors. Over the last two years its ever-evolving FAQs on academy conversion have been consulted by many thousands of governors looking for full and objective guidance as to whether conversion to academy status would be good for their schools. Members will also find briefing papers on topical issues and new legislation, guidance documents on aspects of the governor's role, and useful resources, such as a skills audit template. Publications include the long-established *Welcome to Governance*, a comprehensive guide to the role for new governors.

Each year the NGA holds at least one conference for its members, and generally two, at which national figures talk about their plans and policies and members can express their own opinions.

Representation

Why do governors need representation? This is not our livelihood, nor is there a single political outlook that encompasses all governors. However, a lot of the educational legislation and official guidance affects how we govern our schools. The governors' view of the practicality and effectiveness of these is very important. The NGA responds to scores of consultations each year, and in addition meets with government ministers, civil servants and leaders of government agencies like Ofsted and the National College to make sure that the governors' voice is heard.

In turn, the association needs to ascertain what members themselves think. This is done in part through the NGA board, which consists of 18 trustees, elected by the membership, and in part by talking to governors at local conferences and at the NGA's own events. It also comes through inviting members to fill in questionnaires and a quick and easy monthly on-line questionnaire on the website. One of the most important ways of conducting these soundings is through twice-yearly regional meetings of governors at which all governors from the region, especially those leading governor associations, can share experiences. It is significant in this respect that each of the nine regions elects a member of the NGA's board (the other trustees are elected by the membership at large).

Promoting governance

Most of us became governors because of some desire to help in the education of children. The NGA's aims are basically the same, expressed in its Memorandum of Association as "the improvement of educational welfare of children through the promotion of high standards in schools, colleges and other educational institutions; and the raising of the effectiveness of governing bodies of such institutions". Much of this work is done through the publications already discussed, but it also involves working with other organisations, often by endorsing their work, as with the two national providers of e-training for governors, Modern Governor and GEL (Governors' E-Learning). Support does not stop at endorsement: the NGA will have often contributed to these resources, and also to other organisations supporting governance.

It has been a key partner for the National College in developing support for chairs of governors, jointly publishing a guide for chairs, inputting into the training course for new chairs, and promoting the National Leaders of Governance. It acts as the secretariat to the All Party Parliamentary Group on Governance, in which various MPs and peers of all political parties collaborate to help promote good school governance.

Membership is open to governing bodies, individuals, local authority governor associations (most of which are in membership of the NGA) and corporate bodies. Individual governing bodies in local associations are not themselves automatically members of the NGA, but their associations receive a full range of benefits for their officers.

The need for quality support for governing bodies is growing all the time, as free services from the public purse become increasingly constrained by budget restrictions. As a not-for-profit, charitable organisation, the NGA is a unique position to supply this.

STEPHEN ADAMSON, CHAIR OF THE NGA

In brief

The National Curriculum

In summer 2012 the government published its draft National Curriculum programmes of study for English, maths and science in primary schools, which emphasise children mastering the basics. At the same time the government said it would abolish the NC levels. New programmes of study are to be ready for delivery in schools from September 2014.

National Professional Qualification for Headteachers

From early 2012 the NPQH ceased to be a mandatory qualification for first-time headteachers, though schools may continue to make possession of it an essential criterion when appointing heads if they wish.

Homework guidance goes

Previously governments have published guidelines on how long pupils ought to spend on homework, but these were removed by the Secretary of State in March 2012, leaving the matter up to headteachers. Academic research suggests that the value of homework to primary school children is "inconclusive" and is limited for secondary school pupils

Recruiting governors online

The School Governors' One-Stop Shop (SGOSS) now provides a free online service for schools wishing to recruit new governors. It can be accessed on www.sgoss.org.uk/schools.

Guide to the Law

A new edition of *The Governors' Guide to the Law* was published on line in May 2012, bringing it up to date. The change of title from the longer predecessor (*A Guide to the Law for School Governors*) presages a new approach to the Guide, as at the time of publication it was announced that the next edition would be much simpler and briefer.

SEN changes on the way

The Queen's Speech in May 2012 contained no specific new education legislation, but its Children and Families Bill promises changes to the way the needs of children with Special Educational Needs or disabilities will be met. The three categories of special need – School Action, School Action Plus and statementing – will be replaced in 2014 by a single assessment process and, where deemed appropriate, an Education, Health and Care Plan. Parents of children given an EHCP will have control of the child's personal budget.

part two

PLANNING AND RESOURCES

2013

The governing body

Maintained schools

A governing body in existence before 1 September 2012 can maintain its existing constitution, which was determined by the regulations put in place in 2003. According to these the categories of governor relate to who elected or appointed them: Parent, Community (co-opted by the governing body), Authority (appointed by the local authority), Staff, Teacher (Wales only), Foundation/Partnership (not applicable to community schools) or Sponsor. In England there is only one category of staff governor, but Wales has separate teacher and support staff governors.

One of the staff places in England is reserved for the headteacher (whether they take it up on not), the second must be filled by a teacher (unless no teachers want to stand), and the third (if the governing body is not so small as to only have two staff places) should be filled by a member of the support staff.

In England the governing body will have fixed a size of between 9 (10 in a voluntary aided school) and 20, including the headteacher's place. The proportion of governors from each category is determined, with some flexibility, by the overall size of the governing body. In addition secondary schools may have up to four sponsor governors and primaries two. In Wales the size of the governing body and the number of governors in each category is determined by the overall size and category of the school.

Under new regulations that came into effect on 1 September 2012 governing bodies in England may, if they wish, change their constitutions, with considerable choice over their size and make-up. A minimum of seven governors is specified, but no maximum. Each governing body must have two elected parent members, the headteacher, a local authority governor and a staff governor. All additional governors are coopted by the governing body. The headteacher may chose not take up their place, but if so is entitled at any time to change their mind. The governing body may lay down necessary skills required of a local authority governor, and veto the local authority's choice of individual if he or she does not meet them. See pages 13–15 for more information on the new regulations.

Any governing bodies of maintained schools forming after 1 September 2012 will have do so under the provisions of the 2012 regulations.

Academies

In academies, including Free Schools, the trust or sponsor (in the case of sponsor academies) establishes the governing body, which can be of any size from three up, but around 15 is recommended. The only compulsory places are two parent governors and the principal. The DfE publishes model Articles of Association which allow for a number of governors appointed by the trust, an optional governor from the local authority, optional staff governors (with a maximum equivalent to one third of the governing body), the minimum two parent governors, and up to three co-opted governors appointed by the governing body. Schools that wish to retain their current governing body may usually do so, but if this involves a structure that is different from those in the model Articles of Association, they have to apply for permission from the Secretary of State. Usually with sponsor academies the sponsor will chair the governing body.

Some of the decisions that reside with a governing body of a maintained school are the prerogative of the trust of an academy. The trust sets the ethos and the general strategic direction of the school, while the governing body, as the executive body of the trust, oversees the day-to-day management and operation of the school. See pages 18–20.

Committees

The governing body can have whatever committees it wants, or none. They commonly divide into those handling finance, the curriculum, staff and pupils, but premises, Special Educational Needs, extended services and other subjects may be handled by separate committees or be included in the terms of reference of others.

Either two or three governors must be appointed to conduct the headteacher's performance management review in a maintained school. They have to be supported by an external adviser. Academies may follow the same procedure.

Governing bodies may appoint non-governors as associate members to serve on committees, with voting rights. They may also attend the full governing body meetings if the governing body so decides, but cannot vote.

Appeals and exclusions panels

There should also be governors in readiness to hear staff appeals, parental complaints and consider pupil exclusions.

A member of staff given notice of dismissal, or refused a pay spine point increase or promotion across the threshold, has the right to appeal to a panel of at least three governors. It is advisable to appoint a committee at the start of the school year in readiness, or to establish a list of those willing to serve on one that can be drawn on if necessary.

Similarly it is not a requirement to have a fixed panel to deal with exclusions or the governor stage of parental complaints, but if not it is advisable to establish lists of governors from which to draw members to deal with these if and when required. When formed, each panel should have three or five members, plus an independent clerk. Guidance on both exclusions and complaints is available on the DfE website.

Governing bodies of schools that are admissions authorities must also set up panels to hear appeals against admission decisions. This includes all academies.

Annual workplan

The planner on the next few pages should help you plan your activities for the coming year. It consists of lists of the main governing body tasks, organised by term, together with some special tasks or events. The lists of tasks are divided into the four categories that cover most governing body activity: Finance (including premises); Curriculum and Achievement; Pupils, Families and the Community; and Staffing (personnel).

Governing bodies in England may delegate most of their decision-making powers either to committees or to individuals, within certain restraints. Those things that cannot be delegated to an individual, only to a committee, are the alteration or discontinuance of the school, a change of category of school, approval of the first formal budget plan of the financial year, the determination of admission arrangements or the admission of a particular child, school discipline policies and the exclusion of pupils. On the other hand, governing bodies must delegate to panels or committees the hearing of appeals on pupil discipline, staff dismissals and decisions on staff pay and promotion.

Where delegation is to an individual, in practice this will probably mean the headteacher/principal, or to one or two governors, possibly including the headteacher/principal.

The only items that can only be dealt with by the full governing body are those which relate to the constitution of the governing body itself, such as reconstituting the governing body under the 2012 regulations, the election or removal of the chair or vice chair, co-option of governors, choice and terms of references of committees, appointment of the clerk, and suspension of governors. The governing body may also decide whether to have associate members on committees and whether they can attend full governing body meetings.

In the following lists items in **bold** type are ones which *have* to be considered each year. For most of these, regulations do not state when they should be done, but we have placed them in what is generally regarded the best term for them. Some tasks can be performed at any particular time of the school year, and these are listed on the next page.

TIMING OF RESIGNATIONS

If they want to leave, headteachers and deputies have to hand in their resignations by certain dates in each term.

	Heads	Deputies
To leave at the end of the autumn term:	30 September	31 October
To leave at the end of the spring term:	31 January	28 February
To leave at the end of the summer term:	30 April	31 May

Items to be addressed at the first meeting of the year
Full governing body
Review the range of committees in place and their terms of reference. Elect members and appoint clerks to committees and either elect chairs or agree to delegate this to each committee. Review governor monitoring links

Appoint governors to specific responsibilities as required: training and links with LA governor services, child protection, gifted and talented pupils, SEN

Review individual governors' curriculum/faculty/class responsibilities

Discuss operating guidelines for the governing body

Set objectives of the governing body for the year, linked to SDP

Agree a programme of meetings for the year, including committees

Elect chair and vice chair (academies)

All committees
Elect chair (if not done by full governing body)

Examine School Development/Improvement Plan

Items that may be undertaken at any time
Elect chair and vice chair, if their term of office has expired (maintained schools usually at first meeting of year)

Preparation of Annual Report to Parents for nursery schools and for all schools in Wales (but must be by 31 July each school year)

Updating of school's self-evaluation

Appointment of clerk

Report on any racist incidents and the response, at least annually

Items that should be done on a regular basis
Monitor School Development/Improvement Plan (all committees)

Review/write new policies. Draw up framework for policy review (all committees)

Reports on training attended by governors and discussion of training needed (full GB)

Receive reports:
>from the headteacher/principal (termly) (full GB)
>from committees (full GB)
>on governors' visits to the school (full GB)
>on parental complaints (without details) and outcomes (PFC com.)
>on incidents of bullying and racism, and the responses (PFC com.)
>from the governor/committee with responsibility for SEN (PFC com.)
>from individual governors and staff on their curriculum areas (Curr. com.)
>from the designated teacher for looked-after children (PFC com.)

Review pupil progress and attainment (Curr. com.)

Items that should be included on each agenda
Declaration of pecuniary interests

Receive and consider apologies

Autumn term

For full governing body
If the school is an admissions authority (foundation and VA schools) draw up admissions policy for the next school year

Initiate review of the School Development/Improvement Plan

Update register of pecuniary interests

Issue statement on use of School Premium

Finance
Monitor budget

Review charging policy

Appoint governor(s) for Health & Safety

Complete asset management plan

Staffing
Review Performance Management Policy

Conduct head's performance management review (by 31 December) – advisable to conduct the principal's performance review for an academy

Review and determine the head's/principal's salary (backdated to 1 September) – advisable to determine the principal's pay for an academy

Ensure every teacher has a performance review and that their salary is reviewed by 31 October (backdated to 1 September)

Curriculum and achievement
Review National Curriculum test, GCSE and other exam results

Pupils, families and the community
Receive annual report on safeguarding children

Review net capacity of the school

Plus items listed on previous page

To note
September New parents to be sent Home-School Agreements
Schools in England to set attendance targets for pupils
New Early Years Foundation Stage framework comes into effect
Requirement to publish a paper-based school prospectus abolished
Details of use of Pupil Premium to be published
Start of financial year for academies
Nominations open for NGA Governing Body of the Year and Clerk of the Year awards

October Admissions applications to secondary schools close (31st)

Spring term

For full governing body
Finalise School Development/Improvement Plan

Publish proposed admissions arrangements for autumn of the next year (schools which are admission authorities)

Finance
Review whole school pay policy

Start work on drafting budget for the coming year (maintained schools)

Review charging and letting policy (together with PFC committee)

Review insurance

Staffing
Review staff pay policy

Review staff structure

Curriculum and achievement
SEN report

Report on curriculum developments

Finalise any curriculum plans for coming year

Pupils, families and the community
Publish next edition of school prospectus (or in summer term)

Review charging and letting policy (together with Finance committee)

Assess impact of measures taken to promote community cohesion

Review SEN policy

To note
January Admissions applications to primary schools close (around 15th, may vary in different local authorities)

March National offer day for places at secondary schools (1st)
Maintained schools to be given their budget figures for next financial year
Schools Financial Value Standard (maintained schools) to be submitted to local authority by end of the month
Presentation of NGA Governing Body of the Year and Clerk of the Year awards

Summer term

For full governing body
Conduct self-review of governing body effectiveness

Finance
Agree budget for the new financial year (maintained schools)

Draft budget for new school year (academies)

Audit school fund

Staffing
Review staff pay and provide all teaching staff with details of the statement of their position on the salary spine effective from 1 September (maintained schools – advisory for academies)

Review Performance Management policy (maintained schools – advisory for academies)

Review job descriptions

Review staff attendance

Appoint governors to conduct head's performance review in the autumn, ensure they are or will be trained, and appoint external adviser

Curriculum and achievement
Review and monitor specified curriculum area

Review progress with the School Development/Improvement Plan

Pupils, Families and the Community
Review child protection policy and procedures

Report to parents on the policy for children with SEN (not special schools)

Review attendance of pupils

Review pupil exclusions for the year

Receive report on progress in implementing accessibility plan

To note
April Start of financial year (maintained schools)
Updated information on meeting an objective under the Equalities Act to be published
Schools that are admissions authorities to publish online their entry arrangements (by 1 May)

May Last date (31st) for announcing any proposed redundancies to take effect from September

Essential documents

For all governors

The clerk and chair should ensure governors either receive the following in hard copy or electronic form as they are published, or are notified of where they can be accessed.

Staffing structure, showing all staff and their responsibilities
The school's mission statement and SD/IP
School prospectus information
The school's calendar for the year
Dates of governors' meetings (if not in school calendar)
Details of governor training programme from the local authority
The Home-School Agreement
School and governor newsletters and similar publications sent to parents
Approved budget
The latest report from any improvement professional contracted by the
    school (LA report in Wales)
The latest Ofsted (Estyn in Wales) report
The latest edition of the DfE's *The Governors' Guide to the Law* (main-
    tained schools) or, when published, its *Academies Handbook* (academies).

For new governors

The clerk should give new governors the items in the list above, plus:

Minutes of the previous two governing body meetings
Names and contact details of every governor
Committee structure
The school's Instrument of Government (maintained schools) or Funding
    Agreement (academies)
A small floor plan of the school
Guidance notes on visiting the school
Details of induction training
Start Here (Adamson Publishing) and/or *Welcome to Governance* (NGA)

Documents the governing body should receive from the headteacher/principal

Reports on any school improvement visits
The RAISEonline report (key points to all governors; England)
Budget reports presented in an appropriate format
Regular updates by section of the school self-evaluation
Final version of the Annual Report (Wales; nursery schools in England)

For clerks
(a) When first appointed
All those items given to new governors, plus

Clear written job description

Letter of appointment giving appointment start date

A contract of appointment (statement of particulars) within eight weeks of the commencement date

Up-to-date records relating to the governing body, including
- appointment date of all governors
- contact details (daytime and evening) for every governor and associate member
- membership of committees and working parties, including associate members
- archive of governing body and committee meeting minutes
- the register of governors' attendance at governing body meetings
- list of useful contact names and addresses at the local authority and diocese where appropriate

Any guidance notes on the role of the clerk published by the local authority, DfE (WG in Wales), NGA (or GovernorsWales) or diocese where appropriate

Next local provision of the National Training Programme for Clerks or other locally provided training opportunities for clerks

In church schools, copies of any diocesan or national requirements

(b) On a regular basis
Items for the agenda of governing body meetings

The title and date of documents received from the local authority, DfE (WG in Wales), or diocese where relevant, so they can be listed on the agenda for the next governing body meeting

School newsletters and similar publications sent to parents

Committee minutes, reports and papers to be circulated with the agenda for the governing body meeting (at least one week before)

Details of training opportunities for clerks and governors

(c) When they occur
A copy of the appointment letter sent to each governor by the body appointing them, or the notice of their election

Resignation or notice of withdrawal of appointment for each governor as relevant

Notice of appeal by a parent against an exclusion

All correspondence relating to hearings and appeals, including the notice of appeal against the governors' upholding of the exclusion of a pupil

Correspondence relating to governors' hearings and appeal committees

Any special request to convene an extraordinary meeting of the governing body – to come from at least three governors and be in writing

For governing body and committee chairs

Governing body chairs on a regular basis

Draft minutes of each governing body meeting within 10 days so they can be issued within two weeks of the meeting

Direct mailings from the DfE (WG in Wales), NGA (or GovernorsWales), local authority, and diocese where applicable

Minutes of governing body committees and working parties as soon as they become available

New governing body chairs

Terms of reference of all the committees

The governing body's complaints policy

The school's Performance Management policy

The most recent settlement on the headteacher's/principal's pay

School Teachers' Pay and Conditions Document (DfE), which provides the statutory responsibilities of the head, deputy and other teachers (applies to maintained schools; academies may choose to follow it)

The school's current self-evaluation document and performance data

All current DfE (WG in Wales) and local authority documents that have been sent to the previous chair

Dates of future meetings with the school's improvement professional

Plus any of the documents listed on the previous two pages as necessary for governors and clerks that the chair does not already have

Chairs of committees

Terms of reference for the committee

All NGA (or GovernorsWales), local authority, DfE (or WG) and other publications (and diocesan for church schools) relevant to the work of their committee

The school policies relating to their responsibilities

What should be available for all governors to consult

Governors should know where they can see the following, either in hard copy form or on websites, or whether they are in emails that can be forwarded to them:

All the school's policies

Terms of reference of all committees

The school's current self-evaluation document

Bulletins, guidance notes, etc, from the local authority and NGA

Circulars and relevant documents from the DfE (WG in Wales)*

Relevant books, magazines and newspaper articles

Details of staff INSET (In Service Training) programmes so that, where appropriate and with agreement, governors may be able to attend

* It is helpful if the clerk lists on the agenda for each meeting of the governing body all relevant documents received since the last meeting.

Compliance with statutory regulations

The following list is based on one that was originally produced by Ofsted for inclusion in the school's self-evaluation form. It has been updated to reflect current requirements.

The curriculum
1. Every learner receives the full statutory curriculum that the school must provide.
2. The school provides teaching of religious education for all learners in accordance with the locally agreed syllabus (or otherwise, in accordance with relevant prescribed exceptions) and has told parents/carers of the right to withdraw their children.
3. The school provides a daily act of collective worship for all learners and has told parents/carers of the right to withdraw their children and, where applicable, sixth formers of their own right to withdraw.
4. The school has a written policy on sex and relationships education, and has made it available to parents/carers.
5. *(Schools with pupils of primary age)* The governing body has decided whether or not to provide sex and relationships education (other than that required by the national curriculum) and, if doing so, has agreed the content and organisation of the programme and has told parents/carers about it and the right to withdraw their children.
6. *(Schools with pupils of secondary age)* The governing body has agreed the content and organisation of its programme of sex and relationships education (other than that required by the national curriculum) and has told parents/carers about it and the right to withdraw their children.
7. The school meets fully the learning and development requirements of the Early Years Foundation Stage.

Equality & diversity
8. Under the terms of the Equality Act 2010 and subsequent regulations, governing bodies are required to draw up equality objectives every four years and annually publish information demonstrating how they are meeting the aims of the general public sector equality duty.

Learners with learning difficulties and/or disabilities
9. The school meets its requirements in Part IV of the Education Act 1996 and has regard to the Special Educational Needs Code of Practice when meeting learners' special educational needs, publishes its policy and makes it known to parents/carers and reports annually on the success of its policy.

10. The school meets the requirements of Part 4 of the Disability Discrimination Act 1995 (DDA) and any subsequent requirements and has regard to the (DRC) code of practice for schools (2002). The school informs parents/carers of its accessibility plan and disability equality scheme and reports annually on progress made on these.

11. The school has appointed a special educational needs coordinator and has ensured that the post holder has received training.

Learners' care and well-being

12. The school has procedures in place to ensure it meets all relevant health and safety legislation.

13. The school has a child protection policy and procedures in place that are in accordance with local authority guidance and DfE guidance and locally agreed inter-agency procedures (and the policy is made available to parents/carers on request).

14. Where the governing body provides school lunches and/or other school food, they ensure that they meet current DfE standards (does not apply to academies).

15. If relevant, the school complies with the welfare requirements of the Early Years Foundation Stage.

16. If relevant, the school complies with its duties under section 29 of the Education Act 2011 in the provision of independent careers education, information and advice for pupils in years 9–11. (Applies to maintained schools only, but academies will have similar stipulations in their Funding Agreements.)

Informing parents/carers

17. The headteacher and/or governing body as appropriate ensures that all statutory assessments are conducted and results are forwarded to parents/carers and appropriate bodies.

18. The headteacher (of a maintained school only) ensures that each year a report on each learner's educational achievements is forwarded to their parents/carers.

19. The school keeps parents/carers and prospective parents/carers informed by publishing information on SATS or GCSE results, admission arrangements, the school's ethos and values, the most recent Ofsted report, the charging and behaviour policies, information on the school's curriculum, and details of how the school meets the needs of children with SEN. This information must either be published on the school's website, or the website must indicate where it can be found.

20. The school publishes information on the amount of Pupil Premium the school has received for the current academic year, details of how it is intended that the allocation will be spent, details of how the previous academic year's allocation was spent, and the effect of this expenditure on the educational attainment of those pupils at the school in respect of whom the Pupil Premium was allocated.

Leadership and management

21. The governing body of a maintained school completes the Schools Financial Value Standard and submits it to the local authority by 31 March each year.

22. The responsibilities of the governing body, its committees, the head-teacher/principal and staff in respect of finances are clearly defined and limits of delegated authority are delineated.

23. The governing body of a maintained school has a performance management policy and ensures that all teachers, including the headteacher, are appraised in accordance with statutory requirements.

24. The governing body of a maintained school has secured that the provisions in the School Teachers' Pay and Conditions Document and any associated regulations relating to terms and conditions, including performance management and induction, have been implemented for all teachers and the headteacher.

25. The governing body has all relevant complaints and appeals procedures, as set out for maintained schools in the DfE Guide to the Law for School Governors and for academies in The Education (Independent School Standards) Regulations 2010.

26. The school meets the current government requirements regarding safeguarding children and safer recruitment, including maintaining a central record of recruitment and vetting checks.

27. The governing body ensures that childcare not provided directly by the school is registered, where this is required by the Childcare Act 2006, and complies with all necessary registration requirements.

Guidance on statutory policies and documents is also provided on the DfE website, www.education.gov.uk >Schools>Leadership and governance>Statutory guidance for schools. See also pages 28–30.

School types

Academies are publicly funded independent schools. Unlike other publicly funded schools, they are totally independent of local authorities and receive their funds from central government. They set their own pay and conditions for staff, do not have fully to follow the National Curriculum, and can determine their term dates and the length of their school days. Their land and buildings are owned by a trust. The trust also appoints the governing body, which is subject to looser constitutional rules than maintained schools: academy governing bodies only have to have two parent governors and the principal; all other governors are optional.

There are two routes to academy status. *Converter* academies have chosen to become academies, while conversion to *sponsor* academy status is directed by the Secretary of State for Education or the local authority, usually because of poor academic results. Sponsor academies are supported by another institution, which might be a university, further education college, other school, or trust that runs other academies ("chains"). See also p. 16.

Free Schools are independent schools funded by the state that have been set up in response to parental demand. Free Schools have academy status and hence the same independence. Parents, charities, businesses or groups of teachers may set them up. However, they will not run them – the schools will have governing bodies. Free Schools may be set up in existing, adapted buildings such as offices.

Maintained schools are state-funded schools that are under the responsibility of their local authorities. There are four types: community schools, voluntary aided schools, voluntary controlled schools, and foundation schools (including trust schools).

Community schools are those whose premises are owned by the local authority, which also legally employs the staff and determines admissions arrangements. This is the largest category of schools in the country.

Both **voluntary aided** and **voluntary controlled** schools are varieties of faith school, and are usually closely linked to a Church or other religion. In the case of voluntary aided schools the Church, or religious charity, owns the premises, is responsible for paying 10 percent of the capital costs, and appoints a majority of the governors. The premises of voluntary controlled schools may be owned by a charity, but the local authority pays all the capital costs and is legally the employer of the staff, and only a minority of governors are appointed by the Church or charity. The local authority also determines the admissions arrangements, which are controlled by the governing body in voluntary aided schools.

The premises of **foundation** schools are held on trust by a foundation, a "foundation body" or by the governing body. Foundation schools are more independent of the local authority than community schools, particularly with regards to legally being the employer of the staff, and setting the admissions criteria for the school. However, the school has to follow the national pay rates for staff, teach the National Curriculum, and follow the local authority's term dates. Local authorities have the power to intervene in them if they consider that their standards are not adequate.

Studio schools are small schools (around 300 pupils) for 14- to 19-year-olds that are designed to prepare them for the world of work. They deliver the National Curriculum but together with or in the form of enterprise-themed projects, with a strong emphasis on practical work. The first of them opened in 2010. Studio schools may be part of an existing maintained school or academy, or may be set up as a free-standing academy.

Teaching schools can be any type of state school. They play a leading role in providing and assuring initial teacher training (ITT) in their area and offer other schools professional development for their teachers and leaders. Only schools judged outstanding by Ofsted are eligible to be teaching schools. Designation is usually for four years.

Trust schools are foundation schools supported by a trust (some foundation schools do not have them). The trust is the body that owns the school's premises. A single trust may own the land for several schools, and the schools usually then work closely together. The trust may have a particular ethos, such as a religious one. The term "trust school" is often used for what is referred to in legislation as a "qualifying foundation school", which is one where the trust appoints the majority of governors, rather than following the model for foundation schools. In such cases the governing body only has one elected parent governor.

University Technical Colleges are a new development in education. They are open to 14- to 19-year-olds, and specialise in technical qualifications. Their courses combine academic and practical studies. Each college is sponsored by a university. In June 2012 32 UTCs had been approved to pre-opening stage, two were already open and three were due to open in 2012 and 2013.

Federations and **collaborations** are groups of schools that have agreed to work together in order to improve the education and opportunities offered to their children. Collaborations – sometimes called soft federations –are loose structures, held together by consent, with each school retaining its own governing body. Federations have entered a formal, legally binding agreement as set down in statute. They have a single governing body for all the schools, but each school remains a separate legal entity. Each school can retain its headteacher, but it is quite common for them to have a single head or to have an executive headteacher above the individual heads.

How academies differ from maintained schools

In most respects, governing an academy does not differ from governing a maintained school (especially a foundation or VA school). However, there are some differences in both the constitution of academy governing bodies, which affect their powers, and in their responsibilities.

Every academy has a **trust**, which in law operates the academy and is the leaseholder or freeholder of the land and buildings of the academy. The trust appoints the governors (see pages 18–19), and is responsible for setting the strategic direction of the school. A trust may limit its involvement to determining the ethos of the school and general oversight, or may, especially in an academy chain, take on all governing body responsibilities and leave the local governing body in an advisory capacity – see page 19.

The trust is the **employer** of the staff, but the handling of employment resides with the governing body. Academies are not obliged to follow the national school teachers' pay scales, so governing bodies have discretion over pay (though most stick to the national rates), subject to TUPE rules.

Not all those who **teach** in academies have to be officially qualified to do so, as is the case in maintained schools.

The governing body is financially and practically responsible for the use and maintenance of the academy's **premises**, including health and safety.

Academies do not have to follow the **National Curriculum,** but must offer a broad and balanced curriculum including English, maths, science and IT.

An academy (like a foundation or VA school) is its own **admissions** authority. It can change its catchment area, subject to consultation.

Academies set their own **term dates**, though they must like other schools teach their pupils 195 days of the year.

Academy **financial years** run from 1 September to 31 August. Academies are not allowed to run **deficits,** and do not get supported by the local authority if they run into financial problems.

There are various expenses which are incurred by academies, which for maintained schools may be paid by local authorities. These include redundancy payments to staff, audits of school accounts, education welfare, insurance, support with pupil behaviour, support for specific groups of pupils (such as ethnic minorities) and external educational provision (such as music tuition).

There are costs currently devolved to all schools which maintained schools often buy back from their LAs, such as payroll administration, finance support, HR support and legal services. Academies can also buy these, or any other services, from LAs.

Ofsted's key characteristics of outstanding governing bodies

In May 2011 Ofsted published the findings of a study of 14 governing bodies that inspectors had rated outstanding. The following is the report's summary of features it found they had in common.

- Positive relationships between governors and school leaders are based on trust, openness and transparency. Effective governing bodies systematically monitor their school's progress towards meeting agreed development targets. Information about what is going well and why, and what is not going well and why, is shared. Governors consistently ask for more information, explanation or clarification. This makes a strong contribution to robust planning for improvement.

- Governors are well informed and knowledgeable because they are given high-quality, accurate information that is concise and focused on pupil achievement. This information is made accessible by being presented in a wide variety of formats, including charts and graphs.

- Outstanding governors are able to take and support hard decisions in the interests of pupils: to back the head teacher when they need to change staff, or to change the head teacher when absolutely necessary.

- Outstanding governance supports honest, insightful self-evaluation by the school, recognising problems and supporting the steps needed to address them.

- Absolute clarity about the different roles and responsibilities of the head-teacher and governors underpins the most effective governance. Protocols, specific duties and terms of reference are made explicit in written documents.

- Effective governing bodies are driven by a core of key governors such as the chair and chairs of committees. They see themselves as part of a team and build strong relationships with the headteacher, senior leaders and other governors.

- In eight of the 14 schools visited, governors routinely attend lessons to gather information about the school at work. All the governors who were interviewed visit their schools regularly and talk with staff, pupils and parents. Clear protocols for visits ensure that the purpose is understood by school staff and governors alike. Alongside the information they are given about the school, these protocols help them to make informed decisions, ask searching questions and provide meaningful support.

- School leaders and governors behave with integrity and are mutually supportive. School leaders recognise that governors provide them with a different perspective which contributes to strengthening leadership. The questions they ask challenge assumptions and support effective decision-making.

- Governors ... use the skills they bring, and the information they have about the school, to ask challenging questions, which are focused on improvement, and hold leaders to account for pupils' outcomes.

- Time is used efficiently by governors because there are clear procedures for delegating tasks, for example to well organised committees. These committees have clear terms of reference, provide high levels of challenge and use governors' expertise to best effect. Systems are in place for sharing information and reporting back to the full governing body. This does not merely reiterate what has already been discussed in detail by the committee but focuses on the key points and decisions.

- The role of the clerk to the governors is pivotal to ensuring that statutory duties are met, meetings are well organised and governors receive the information they need in good time. Consequently, governors come to meetings well prepared and with pertinent questions ready so that they are able to provide constructive challenge.

- A detailed timeline of activities, maintained by the clerk and linked to the school development plan, provides a clear structure for the work of governors and ensures that their time is used appropriately.

- Governors ... use their external networks and professional contacts to fill any identified gaps in the collective skills of the governing body.

- There are clear induction procedures for new governors which help them to understand their roles and responsibilities and ensure that best use is made of their varied skills and expertise.

- The governing bodies constantly reflect on their own effectiveness and readily make changes to improve. They consider their own training needs, as well as how they organise their work.

School Governance: Learning from the best, Ofsted, May 2011

Twenty key questions

The following questions have been drawn up by the All Party Parliamentary Group on Governance to help a school governing body assess itself.

Right skills: Do we have the right skills on the governing body?
1. Have we completed a skills audit of our governing body?
2. Do we appoint governors on the basis of their skills, and do we know how to find people with the necessary skills?

Effectiveness: Are we as effective as we could be?
3. Do we understand our roles and responsibilities?
4. Do we have a professional clerk and run meetings efficiently?
5. What is our training and development budget and does every governor receive the support they need to carry out their role effectively?
6. Do we know about good practice from across the country?
7. Are the size, composition and committee structure of our governing body conducive to effective working?
8. Does every member of the governing body make a regular contribution and do we carry out an annual review of the governing body's performance?

Strategy: Does the school have a clear vision?
9. Have we developed long-term aims for the school with clear priorities in an ambitious school development plan which is regularly monitored and reviewed?
10. Does our strategic planning and reviewing cycle drive the governing body's activities and agenda setting?

Accountability of the executive: Do we hold the school leaders to account?
11. Do we understand the school's performance data well enough to properly hold school leaders to account?
12. How effective is our performance management of the headteacher?
13. Are our financial management systems robust and do we ensure best value for money?

Engagement: Are we properly engaged with our school community, the wider school sector and the outside world?
14. How do we listen to and understand our pupils, parents and staff?
15. How do we report to our parents and local community regularly?
16. What benefit do we draw from collaboration with other schools and other sectors, locally and nationally?

Role of chair: Does our chair show strong and effective leadership?
17. Do we carry out an regular 360 review of the chair's performance?
18. Do we engage in good succession planning?
19. Are the chair and committee chairs re-elected each year?

Impact: Are we having an impact on outcomes for pupils?
20. How much has the school improved over the last three years, and what has the governing body's contribution been to this?

The floor standards

For both primary and secondary schools there are three measures set by government to ascertain whether they are delivering sufficiently high standards. To be judged as below the floor, a school has to fail to meet *all three*.

For **primary schools** these have been set at:

- 60 percent of pupils achieving at least level 4 in English and maths at Key Stage 2
- the national average percentage of pupils making expected progress in English by the end of Key Stage 2 (the national median for 2011 was 85%)
- the national average percentage of pupils making expected progress in maths by the end of Key Stage 2 (the national median for 2011 was 83%).

"Expected progress" is an advance of two National Curriculum levels.

For **secondary schools** the targets are:

- 40 percent of pupils achieving at least five A*–C grade GCSEs, including English and maths (this is the figure for 2012-13; for 2011-12 it was 35 percent)
- the national average percentage of pupils making expected progress in English between the ends of Key Stages 2 and 4 (national median for 2011 was 74%)
- the national average percentage of pupils making expected progress in maths between the ends of Key Stages 2 and 4 (national median for 2011 was 66%).

"Expected progress" is based on advancing from National Curriculum level 4 at the end of Key Stage 2 to at least a GCSE grade C, so also therefore from level 3 to an D grade, or level 5 to a B grade, etc.

The Secretary of State for Education has announced (in June 2011) that he will increase the first secondary-school floor target to 50 percent by 2015.

Schools that fail to meet the floor targets for five consecutive years will be converted into academies.

In 2011 216 secondary schools were below the floor standards and 1310 primary schools.

Governance in Wales

Summary of the main differences from England

Legislation	National Assembly for Wales has full legislative powers on Education following successful Referendum in March 2011
Regulatory bodies	Separate bodies for Wales on Curriculum and Assessment, and Post-16 Education, part of Welsh Government. Separate General Teaching Council (still in operation)
Curriculum	Foundation Phase for 3- to 7-year-olds, based on experiential learning Extra compulsory subject up to KS4 (Welsh; English in Welsh-medium schools) Learning Pathways for 14- to 19-year-olds – to broaden the range of academic, vocational, and work-based courses available Welsh Baccalaureate for 16+ widely available
Assessment and testing	National tests for reading and numeracy to be introduced during 2013 to supplement teacher assessment
League tables	Not in Wales, but banding scheme for secondary school performance in place, and primary school bandings planned for 2014
School governance	Separate regulations; significant differences from England especially on composition of governing bodies, e.g. provision for two associate pupil governors from Y11, 12, or 13 to be nominated through school council (secondary schools) Mandatory training for new governors and new chairs
"Reforms"	No specialist schools, trust schools, academies, or Free Schools Continuing commitment to comprehensive system of education
Inspection	A different regime in Wales, including Inspection body, Estyn
Finance	Education SSA is indicative only. LAs fix funding levels of schools
Teachers' pay	Wales bound by same statutory provision as England, e.g. Teaching and Learning Responsibility payments
Reporting to parents	Governors present an Annual Report to Parents. Education Bill will abolish requirement for an Annual Meeting with Parents unless 10 percent of parents petition for one

The National Curriculum

Subjects in the National Curriculum are divided into core and non-core. The core subjects are compulsory for all pupils in maintained schools.

Core subjects
English, mathematics and science (and Welsh in Wales)

Non-core subjects
ICT, PE – compulsory at all key stages
Art and design, design and technology, geography, history, music – compulsory at KS1–3
Modern foreign languages – compulsory at KS3
Citizenship – compulsory at KS3–4

Religious education is not a core subject but is compulsory. PSHE is not compulsory, but the National Curriculum provides guidance on teaching it. Sex and relationships education is only compulsory at KS3 and 4. At KS4 careers education and work-related learning are compulsory.
The National Curriculum will be reformed in September 2014.

Key Stage	School year	Age of pupil	Type of school	Attainment Level*
Foundation		3–4	Nursery/nursery class/early years	
	Reception	4–5	Primary	
KS1	Year 1	5–6	Infant	Range: 1–3
	Year 2	6–7		Age 7 norm: 2
KS2	Year 3	7–8	Junior	
	Year 4	8–9		
	Year 5	9–10		Range: 2–5
	Year 6	10–11		Age 11 norm: 4
KS3	Year 7	11–12	Secondary	
	Year 8	12–13		Range: 3–7
	Year 9	13–14		Age 14 norm:5/6
KS4	Year 10	14–15		
	Year 11	15–16		
	Year 12	16–17	Secondary; 6th Form College; FE College	
	Year 13	17–18+		

* The first figure given for each Key Stage is the range of levels at which the vast majority of pupils are expected to work. The norm is the expected attainment for the majority of pupils at the end of the Key Stage.

Information sources

In the following, government departments are referred to by their name at the time of publication, e.g. DfE after June 2010, DCSF before June 2010 and DfES before July 2007.

General roles

The Governors' Guide to the Law, DfE, only available online at
   www.education.gov.uk >Leadership and governance
Being Strategic, David Marriott, Adamson Publishing, 3rd edn 2011
Governing Body Decision Planner, DfE website
   (www.education.gov.uk) >Schools>Leadership and
   governance>Governance>Governing body procedures and commit-
   tees>Roles of governing bodies and headteachers
Joined-up Governance, J. Martin & A. Holt, Adamson Publishing, rev.
   edn 2011
GEL (Governors' E-Learning), www.elc-gel.org, on-line training for
   governors
Modern Governor, www.moderngovernor.com, on-line training for
   governors

Academies

General information is available from the Department for Education, www.education.gov.uk/academies.
FAQs for those considering taking on academy status are on the Academies pages of the Department for Education website. Regularly updated advice for governors on converting to an academy is available for NGA members on its website, www.nga.org.uk.
Academies – Understanding the legislative framework, ACE, http://eep-url.com/ntS8b

Accountability

Accountability: A practical guide for school governors, Stephen
   Adamson, Adamson Publishing, 2007

Admissions

School Admissions Code, DfE website (www.education.gov.uk)
   >Schools>Administration and finance>School admissions

Appointing and recruiting staff

A Guide to Recruiting and Selecting a New Headteacher, National College
   in conjunction with the National Governors' Association, www.nga.
   org.uk

Safeguarding Children and Safer Recruitment in Education, DfES, 2006
(DFES-04217-2006)

Recruiting Headteachers and Senior Leaders, National College for
Leadership of Schools and Children's Services,
www.nationalcollege.org.uk, search in Leadership Library

Tomorrow's Leaders Today: A toolkit for governors, National College for
Leadership of Schools and Children's Services, www.nationalcollege.
org.uk//index/leadershiplibrary/leadingschools/toolkit-for-
governors.htm

Bullying

Preventing and Tackling Bullying, DfE, www.education.gov.uk
>Schools>Pupil support>Bullying

Tackling Bullying in Schools: a guide for governors, Anti-Bullying
Alliance, www.abatoolsforschools.org.uk/resources/aba_tools.aspx

No Place for Bullying, Ofsted, www.ofsted.gov.uk/resources/no-place-for-
bullying

Chairing

Leading Governors, NGA and National College, on the National College
website, www.education.gov.uk/nationalcollege

The National College website contains other useful resources for chairs

Charging and school visits

Charging for school activities, DfE, www.education.gov.uk
>Schools>Administration and finance>Schools financial manage-
ment>Good practice

Child protection

Various documents are published on the DfE website,
www.education.gov.uk >Schools>Pupil support> Pastoral care

Christian governors

Transforming Governing, www.transforminggoverning.org.uk, website
for Christians seeking to put their principles into action as governors

Clerks

Welcome to Clerking, NGA, 2009

Clerkwise, on-line information service for clerks, www.adamsonbooks.com

Governors Virtual Office, www.schoolleadershipsystems.com, on-line
tool to manage the governing body's work and communications

For Clerks, section of the GEL website for clerks to governing bodies (see
General Roles)

Complaints

Complaints Procedure Toolkit, DfE, 2012, www.education.gov.uk>Schools
>Leadership and governance>Governance

Computing in Schools

Computing at School (CAS) – www.computingatschool.org.uk.

Curriculum

The DfE website, www.education.gov.uk>Schools>Teaching and learning >The school curriculum gives details of the curriculum for both maintained schools and academies, including the National Curriculum

Data

Knowing Your School, Primary RAISEonline, RM Education and NGA, NGA, 2011

Knowing Your School, Secondary RAISEonline, RM Education and NGA, NGA, 2011

Fischer Family Trust, www.fischertrust.org

RAISEonline, www.raiseonline.org

Department for Education (DfE) www.education.gov.uk Gives information on recent news items and a wide range of guidance documents. The section on Leadership and Governance can be accessed under the heading Schools on the home page, or directly through www.education.gov.uk/schools/leadership. These pages contain the most up-to-date version of *The Governors' Guide to the Law*, as well as many other documents on governance of both maintained schools and academies. The DfE is also on Facebook, www.facebook.com/educationgovuk, Twitter, http://twitter.com/#!/educationgovuk and YouTube, www.youtube.com/user/educationgovuk.

Disability

Disability Discrimination Act Code of Practice for Schools, www.equality-humanrights.com/advice-and-guidance/information-for-advisers/codes-of-practice

Drugs

Drugs: Guidance for schools, DfES, 2004, DfES-0092-2004 (The DfE is planning to replace this guidance)

Equality

Guidance for Education Providers: Schools, Equality and Human Rights Commission, www.equalityhumanrights.com >Advice and guidance

Exclusions

Guidance documents are on the DfE website, www.education.gov.uk >Schools>Pupil support>Behaviour and attendance>Exclusion

ACE (see page 93) runs a helpline on exclusions.

Federation

Guidance on the School Governance (England Federation) Regulations 2007, DfES, on DfE website, www.education.gov.uk >Schools>Leadership and governance>Governance>Collaborations and federations

Finance
Managing School Resources, toolkit from the Audit Commission,
www.schoolresources.audit-commission.gov.uk
See also www.education.gov.uk>Schools>
Administration and finance>Schools financial management
*Academies funding and finance: Academy financial management and
governance evaluation returns* is in the same part of the DfE website

Foundation governors
Foundation Governors: Your own guide, Joan Sallis, Adamson
Publishing, 2006, rev. 2011

Free Schools
New Schools Network, www.newschoolsnetwork.org. Gives advice to
potential suppliers of new schools

Freedom of Information
The Information Commissioner, *www.informationcommissioner.gov.uk*
Guidance and clarification on the Freedom of Information Act

Governing body improvement
School Governance: Learning from the best, Ofsted 2011

Governing body succession
Succession Breeds Success: How to grow leaders in your governing body,
National Co-ordinators of Governor Services/School Governors' One
Stop Shop, www.ncogs.org.uk

> **Governorline** www.education.gov.uk/governorline
> Explains the Governorline helpline service (see page 93) and gives
> advice on problems that are frequently raised by governors.

Headteacher/principals and governors
*Headteachers and Governing Bodies: A practical guide to making the
partnership work*, Martin Pounce, Adamson Publishing, rev. edn 2010
Roles of Governing Bodies and Headteachers, DfE,
www.education.gov.uk>Schools>Leadership and governance
>Governance>Governing body procedures and committees>

Health and safety
Departmental advice on health and safety for schools, DfE, www.educa-
tion.gov.uk>About the department>Departmental advice

> **Governors Wales** www.governorswales.org.uk
> Website for governors in Wales, including the *Governors Wales'
> Handbook*, information about training, fact files, surveys and a chat
> box facility.

Healthy pupils

Healthy Schools toolkit, DfE, www.education.gov.uk>Schools>Pupil
  support>Pastoral care>Pupil health and wellbeing
*Food Policy in Schools – A strategic policy framework for school
  governing bodies*, NGA/Food Standards Agency, 2007

Inspection

*School Self-Evaluation, Improvement and Inspection: A practical guide
  for school governors*, Martin Pounce, Adamson Publishing, 2012
Ofsted, *The Framework for the Inspection of Maintained Schools in
  England,* Ofsted, www.ofsted.gov.uk>Forms and guidance>Education
  and skills>Schools

Insurance

Guidance on Insurance, DfE, www.education.gov.uk>Schools
  >Administration and finance>Emergency planning>Planning for an
  emergency

Learning outside the classroom

Out & About, guidance to help build regular learning-outside-the-class-
  room activities into school lesson plans, www.lotc.org.uk.

Local authority governors

Local Authority Governors: Your own guide, Joan Sallis, Adamson
  Publishing, 2006

Looked after children

Various documents can be found on the DfE website,
  www.education.gov.uk>Children and young people>Families>
  Children in care

Monitoring

Monitoring and Evaluation: A practical guide for school governors,
  David Marriott, Adamson Publishing, 3rd edn 2011

National Governors' Association www.nga.org.uk
The NGA site includes press releases, details of its publications, policy
statements, notices of forthcoming conferences and responses to
national consultations. It also has information about the Association's
work and how to join. The members' section includes guidance
documents, a comprehensive list of FAQs on converting to academy
status and a weekly newsletter on what is happening in education. See
also pages 56–7.

New governors

Start Here: A guide for new governors, Adamson Publishing, rev. edn 2009
Welcome to Governance, NGA, rev. edn 2012

Parent governors
Parent Governors: Your own guide, Joan Sallis, Adamson Publishing,
  2006, rev. 2011

Parent Governor Representatives (PGRs)
An overview is given on the DfE website (www.education.gov.uk)
  >Schools>Leadership and governance>Governance>Becoming a gover-
  nor>Parent governor representatives
The Parent Governor Representatives Network, http://pgr.dcsf.gov.uk

Parents
Achieving Effective Partnerships with Parents (EPPa) Toolkit,
  Southgate Publishers www.southgatepublishers.co.uk
Directgov, www.direct.gov.uk/en/Parents/index.htm Advice for parents
  on choosing schools, school life, SEN and wider parenting matters
Parent View, section of the Ofsted website where parents can answer a
  12-question survey on their views of their child's school, http://par-
  entview.ofsted.gov.uk

Performance management
Teacher Appraisal and Capability – A model policy for schools, DfE,
  www.education.gov.uk >Schools>Leadership and governance
  >Managing and deploying staff>New arrangements for teacher
  appraisal and capability. These pages also give guidance.

Planning
Being Strategic: A practical guide for school governors and headteachers,
  David Marriott, Adamson Publishing, rev. edn 2011

Policies
Policies: A guide for school governors and headteachers, Michele
  Robbins & Martin Baxter, Adamson Publishing, 6th edn 2012

Procurement
Buying Specific goods and Services, DfE, www.education.gov.uk>Schools
  >Administration and finance>Buying goods and services

Pupil behaviour
Various documents, including *Guidance for Governing Bodies on
  Behaviour and Discipline*, can be found on the DfE website, www.
  education.gov.uk>Schools>Pupil support>Behaviour and attendance

Pupil voice
Children's Commissioner for England, www.childrenscommissioner.gov.uk
School Councils UK, www.schoolcouncils.org

Recruitment of governors
School Governors' One-Stop Shop, www.sgoss.org.uk Finds and holds lists
  of people wishing to become governors, and gives advice on governor
  recruitment

Recruitment of staff
See Appointing and recruiting staff

Religious education
Religious education in English schools: Non-statutory guidance 2010, DfE, www.education.gov.uk>Schools>Teaching and learning>The school curriculum

Safeguarding
Independent Safeguarding Authority, www.isa.homeoffice.gov.uk
Safeguarding Children and Safer Recruitment in Education, DCSF, 2006, www.education.gov.uk/publications
See also Child Protection

School details
Schoolsnet, www.schoolsnet.com Lists schools throughout the UK, giving a profile of each
EduBase, http://www.education.gov.uk/edubase/about.xhtml Database of educational establishments across England and Wales, run by the DfE

School Improvement Planning
School Improvement Planning Framework, a suite of tools developed to help schools with their planning and strategic thinking, http://webarchive.nationalarchives.gov.uk/20090219060133/tda.gov.uk/remodelling/extendedschools/sipf2.aspx

School self-evaluation
School Self-Evaluation, Improvement and Inspection: A practical guide for school governors, Martin Pounce, Adamson Publishing, 2012

Special Educational Needs and Disability
SEN/AEN VfM Resource Pack for Schools, http://sen-aen.audit-commission.gov.uk
DfE website, www.education.gov.uk>Children and young people>SEN and disability contains various documents

Staff governors
Staff Governors: Your own guide, Joan Sallis, Adamson Publishing, 2006, rev. 2009

Sustainability
The Green School: How your school can achieve and promote sustainability, Stan Terry, Adamson Publishing, 2008

Teachers' pay
School Teachers' Pay and Conditions Document, on the DfE website (www.education.gov.uk) Schools>Careers and employment>Pay and pensions

Common terms, abbreviations and acronyms

ACE	*Advisory Centre for Education (see page 93)*
ADHD	*Attention Deficit Hyperactivity* Disorder
AfL	*Assessment for Learning*
ALS	*Additional Literacy Support*
APP	*Assessing Pupil's Progress – scheme to help teachers monitor pupils' development*
APPG	*All Party Parliamentary Group on Education Governance and Leadership. Informal group of MPs and peers that meets to discuss how to improve school leadership and governance.*
ASCL	*Association of School and College Leaders*
AST	*Advanced Skills Teacher*
ATL	*Association of Teachers and Lecturers*
AWPU *or* AWPA	*Age-Weighted Pupil Unit or Age Weighted Pupil Allocation – unit used in calculating the funding of the school, weighted according to the pupils' ages.*
BME	*Black and minority ethnic*
BTEC	*Business and Technology Education Council – name also given to the qualifications it awards for vocational courses*
CAF	*Common Assessment Framework – a standardised approach to assessing and meeting a child's additional needs*
Cohort	*Body of pupils entering a school in any one year*
CPD	*Continuing Professional Development*
CRB	*Criminal Records Bureau*
CVA	*Contextual value added (measure previously but no longer used in RAISEonline)*
DfE	*Department for Education*
DSG	*Dedicated Schools Grant – grant from government to fund all of a local authority's Schools Budget expenditure*
EAL	*English as an Additional Language*
EBac/EBacc	*English Baccalaureate, which pupils are deemed to have achieved if they gain A*–C GCSEs in English, maths, geography or history, two sciences and a foreign language*
EBD	*Emotional and Behavioural Difficulties*

ECM	*Every Child Matters*
EFA	*Education Funding Agency – body responsible for the funding of academies, Free Schools and 16-19 provision*
EHCP	*Education and Health Care Plan – support for children with pronounced Special Educational Needs, to come in in 2014*
EMAG	*Ethnic Minority Achievement Grant*
Estyn	*Inspection body for education and training in Wales*
FE	*Further Education*
FTE	*Full Time Equivalent – part-time staff measured according to how many full-time staff would be required to work the same number of hours*
GAG	*General Annual Grant – the funding received each year by an academy*
GCSE	*General Certificate of Secondary Education*
G&T	*Gifted and talented*
GTC	*General Teaching Council of England (now abolished)*
HE	*Higher Education*
HMCI	*Her Majesty's Chief Inspector – the head of Ofsted*
HMI	*Her Majesty's Inspector*
ICT	*Information and Communications Technology*
IEB	*Interim Executive Board. Temporary board of governors appointed by the Secretary of State for Education or the LA to replace the governing body of a failing school*
IEP	*Individual Education Plan*
IiP	*Investors in People*
INSET	*In-Service Training for Teachers*
ISR	*Individual School Range – categorisation of a school according to size and type used in calculating the salary level of a headteacher*
ITT	*Initial Teacher Training*
KS1(2/3/4)	*Key Stage One (Two/Three/Four). The term Key Stage Five is sometimes used to describe the sixth form level.*
LA	*Local Authority*
LADO	*Local Authority Designated Officer – to whom child protection cases involving allegations against school staff and volunteers must be referred*
LSA	*Learning Support Assistant*
LSCB	*Local Safeguarding Children Board*

MLD   *Moderate Learning Difficulties*

NAHT   *National Association of Head Teachers*
NASEN   *National Association for Special Educational Needs*
NASUWT   *National Association of Schoolmasters/Union of Women Teachers*
National College *Shorthand for the National College for Leadership of Schools and Children's Services (see page 95)*
NC   *National Curriculum*
NEET   *Not in education, employment or training*
NFER   *National Foundation for Educational Research*
NGA   *National Governors' Association (see pages 56–7 and 93)*
NLE   *National Leader of Education*
NLG   *National Leader of Governance – an experienced and skilled governor available to help governing bodies in difficulties*
NPQH   *National Professional Qualification for Headship*
NQT   *Newly Qualified Teacher*
NUT   *National Union of Teachers*
NVQ   *National Vocational Qualification*

Ofqual   *Office of the Qualifications and Examinations Regulator*
Ofsted   *Office for Standards in Education, Children's Services and Skills*

PFI   *Private Finance Initiative – scheme whereby a public body such as an LA contracts a private company both to provide a capital asset, like a building, and then to maintain it*
PPA   *Preparation, planning and assessment time – designated non-teaching time for teachers to prepare for lessons and to assess pupils' progress*
PRU   *Pupil Referral Unit. LA-maintained organisation that educates pupils excluded from schools or unable to attend for reasons such as illness.*
PSA   *Parent Support Adviser*
PSHE   *Personal, Social and Health Education*
PSP   *Pastoral Support Plan*
PTA   *Parent Teacher Association*
PTA-UK   *National association for PTAs, previously the National Confederation of Parent Teacher Associations*

QCDA   *Qualifications and Curriculum Development Agency (now closed)*
QTS   *Qualified Teacher Status*

RAISEonline *Reporting and Analysis for Improvement through School Self-Evaluation. On-line data on pupil performance for each school published by Ofsted and DfE*

SACRE *Standing Advisory Council for Religious Education – statutory body of representatives of an LA, religious organisations and teachers, which advises on religious education and worship*

SATs *Standard Assessment Tests – commonly used (though unofficial) name for national tests carried out in England at ages 7 and 14*

SD/IP *School Development/Improvement Plan*

SEAL *Social and Emotional Aspects of Learning*

SEF *Self-Evaluation Form, previously devised by Ofsted for use prior to an inspection. In Wales: School Effectiveness Framework*

SEN *Special Educational Needs*

SENCO *Special Educational Needs Co-ordinator*

SEND *Special Educational Needs and Disabilities*

SFVS *Schools Financial Value Standard*

SGOSS *School Governors' One-Stop Shop – organisation that recruits people interested in becoming governors and then passes on their details to schools looking for governors*

SI *Statutory Instrument*

SLA *Service Level Agreement*

SLD *Severe Learning Difficulties*

SLT *Senior Leadership Team*

STRB *School Teachers' Review Body – group that advises the government on teachers' pay and conditions each year*

TA *Teaching assistant*

TDA *Training and Development Agency for Schools (closed)*

TLR *Teaching and Learning Responsibility – management responsibility for which a teacher receives extra pay*

TUPE *Transfer of Undertakings (Protection of Employment) regulations*

UCAS *Universities and Colleges Admissions Service*

UTC *University Technical College – a new educational institution for 14- to 19-year-olds where they can follow courses in technical subjects*

VA *Voluntary Aided*

VC *Voluntary Controlled*

VfM *Value for Money*

Useful addresses

Organisations for governors and parents

National Governors' Association (NGA)
The national voice for governors in England. Membership is either as a governing body, an individual, or a local-authority-based association of governing bodies. Its aims are to consult and represent governors, provide information and support to governors, and promote high standards in the exercise of governors' responsibilities. 36 Great Charles Street, Birmingham B3 3JY ☎ 0121 237 3780 governorhq@nga.org.uk www.nga.org.uk

Governors Wales
Confederation of school governor associations in Wales, designed to provide support for governors of all schools. Ground floor, 3 Oaktree Court, Mulberry Drive, Cardiff Business Park, Cardiff CF23 8RS ☎ 029 2048 7858 helpline: 0845 602 0100 contact@governorswales.org.uk www.governorswales.org.uk

Advisory Centre for Education (ACE)
ACE "presses for a fairer and more responsive education system" and gives free advice to parents of children in state schools. Issues books and periodicals. United House, North Road, London N7 9DP ☎ 020 7697 1140 enquiries@ace-ed.org.uk www.ace-ed.org.uk
free phone advice: 0808 800 5793 exclusion information: 020 7704 9822

Information for School and College Governors (ISCG)
Provides advice on admissions and exclusions, runs seminars, provides advice to governors and holds a governor sounding panel, and produces the Clerks' Manual. PO Box 3934, Gerards Cross, SL9 1AG ☎ 01483 300280 iscg@governors.uk.com www.governors.uk.com

School Governors' One-Stop Shop Unit 11, Shepperton House, Shepperton Road, London N1 3DF ☎ 020 7354 9805 info@sgoss.org.uk www.sgoss.org.uk

---

Governors' helplines
England: Governorline 08000 722181 www.governorline.co.uk
Wales: Governors Wales 0845 60 20 100
Both take phone calls on any queries relating to school governance between 9am and 10pm on weekdays and between 11am and 4pm at weekends; they are not available on public holidays.

Church organisations

Catholic Education Service 39 Ecclestone Square, London SW1V 1BX
☎ 020 7901 1900 general@cesew.org.uk www.cesew.org.uk

Church of England Education Division Church House, Great Smith
Street, London SW1P 3NZ ☎ 020 7898 1000 webmaster@c-of-e.org.uk
www.churchofengland.org/education.aspx

Government and other national organisations

Advisory, Conciliation and Arbitration Service (ACAS) Euston Tower,
286 Euston Road, London NW1 3JJ ☎ 08457 38 37 36 helpline: 08457
474747 www.acas.org.uk

Association of Directors of Children's Services (ADCS) 3rd Floor, The
Triangle, Exchange Square, Manchester M4 3TR ☎ 0161 838 5757
info@adcs.org.uk www.adcs.org.uk

Audit Commission 1st Floor, Millbank Tower, Millbank, London SW1P
4HQ ☎ 0844 798 3131 www.audit-commission.gov.uk

Children's Services Network (CSN) 22 Upper Woburn Place, London
WC1H 0TB ☎ 020 7554 2800 info@lgiu.org.uk
https://member.lgiu.org.uk/csn/Pages/default.aspx

Department for Education (DfE) Sanctuary Buildings, Great Smith
Street, London SW1P 3BT ☎ 0870 000 2288 e-mail through the
Contact Us page of the website www.education.gov.uk

DfE Publications Centre ☎ 0845 602 2260 Orders from
www.education.gov.uk/publications

Equality and Human Rights Commission (EHRC) *England* 3 More
London, Riverside Tooley Street, London SE1 2RG *and* Arndale House,
Arndale Centre, Manchester M4 3EQ ☎ 0845 604 6610
info@equalityhumanrights.com *Wales* 3rd floor, 3 Callaghan Square,
Cardiff, CF10 5BT ☎ 0845 604 8810 wales@equalityhumanrights.com
www.equalityhumanrights.com

Freedom and Autonomy for Schools – National Association (FASNA)
Represents self-governing schools (where the governing body is the
employer, the admissions authority and the owner of the property).
FASNA Office, Landau Forte College, Fox Street, Derby DE1 2LF
☎ 01332 386769 admin@fasna.org.uk www.fasna.org.uk

HM Inspectorate for Education and Training in Wales (Estyn) Anchor
Court, Keen Road, Cardiff CF24 5JW ☎ 029 2044 6446
enquiries@estyn.gsi.gov.uk www.estyn.gov.uk

Independent Safeguarding Authority (ISA) PO Box 181, Darlington.

DL1 9FA ☎ 01325 953 795 isadispatchteam@homeoffice.gsi.gov.uk
www.isa.homeoffice.gov.uk

Independent Schools Council (ISC) St Vincent House, 30 Orange Street,
London WC2H 7HH ☎ 020 7766 7070 www.isc.co.uk

National College for Leadership of Schools and Children's Services
Triumph Road, Nottingham NG8 1DH ☎ 0845 609 0009 email
through the Contact Us section of the main website: http://www.educa-
tion.gov.uk/nationalcollege members' site: www.nationalcollege.org.uk

Office for Standards in Education, Children's Services and Skills (Ofsted)
Alexandra House, 33 Kingsway, London WC2B 6SE ☎ 08456 404045
enquiries@ofsted.gov.uk www.ofsted.gov.uk

Office of the Qualifications and Examinations Regulator (Ofqual)
Spring Place, Coventry Business Park, Herald Avenue, Coventry CV5
6UB ☎ 0300 303 3344 info@ofqual.gov.uk http://ofqual.gov.uk

Office of the Schools Adjudicator Mowden Hall, Staindrop Road,
Darlington DL3 9BG ☎ 0870 001 2468 osa.team@osa.gsi.gov.uk
www.schoolsadjudicator.gov.uk

Stationery Office, The St Crispins, Duke Street, Norwich NR3 1PD
☎ 0870 600 5522 customer.services@tso.co.uk www.tso.co.uk

Welsh Government, Department for Education and Skills Cathays Park,
Cardiff CF10 3NQ ☎ 0300 060 3300 (English) or 0300 060 4400
(Welsh) wag-en@mailuk.custhelp.com http://new.wales.gov.uk/topics/
educationandskills/?lang=en

Who's Who in Education

Secretary of State for Education	Michael Gove (Con.)
Minister, schools (incl. governance)	Nick Gibb (Con.)
Minister, children & families	Sarah Teather (Lib. Dem.)
Under Secretary, children and families	Tim Loughton (Con.)
Under Secretary, schools (incl. governance)	Lord Hill of Oareford (Con.)
Shadow DfE Secretary	Stephen Twigg
Education and Skills in Welsh Government	Leighton Andrews
Governor associations	
NGA	Emma Knights (CE), Stephen Adamson (chair)
Governors Wales	Jane Morris (director), Terry O'Marah (chair)
Other	
HM Chief Inspector of Schools	Sir Michael Wilshaw
National College	Steve Munby (Chief Exec.)

The names are correct at the time of going to press but can change any time.

Index

abuse of children 54
academy, conversion to 56
academy, governance of 18–20, 75
Admissions Code 28
All Party Parliamentary Group on Governance 78
appointment of headteachers 47–8
appraisal *see* performance management
armed forces 26
Articles of Association 61
aspiration 8
associate members 14
attendance 9

bullying 40

capability 31–4
Chairs of Governors Development Programme 49–50
charitable status 19–20
child welfare 8
clerks, documents for 69
co-operative trust 16–17
co-opted governors 13, 60
committees 61
community governors 13
complaints 61
compliance 12, 70
computing 43–4
converter academies 73
CRB checks 55
creationism 8
curriculum 41–2, 44, 70
curriculum policy 28, 42

data 24–5, 42
data protection 29–30
day of action 8
diplomas 8

Early Years Foundation Stage 9
Education Act 2011 8
Education, Health and Care Plan 58
educational spending 8
English Baccalaureate 23
equality 28, 70
exclusion 51–2

federation 16, 47, 74
Financial Management and Governance Evaluation 29, 36
Fischer Family Trust 24–5
floor standards 79
foundation schools 14, 15, 73

free school meals 26, 35, 52
Free Schools 8, 32, 42, 60, 73
funding 34–5
funding agreements 8

General Teaching Council 31
governance of academies 60, 61
governance, reform of 9
Governorline 85
Governors' Guide to the Law 24, 28, 42, 58, 84
Governors Wales 46, 85

Her Majesty's Chief Inspector of Schools 8, 10, 31–2, 40, 95
homework 9, 58

ICT 43–4
independent review panel 51
Independent Safeguarding Authority 54–5
Individual School Range 48
induction documents 67
infant class size 35
information, publishing 44, 71
inspection 10–12

liability, governors' 20
Local Authority Central Spend Equivalent Grant 35
Local Authority Designated Officer 55
local authority governors 13, 60
local governing body 19
looked after children 52

multi-academy trust 17, 18, 47

National College 49–50
National Curriculum 41, 42, 58, 75, 81; review 8, 9
National Governors' Association 50, 56–7, 86
National Leaders of Governance 50
National Professional Qualification for Headteachers 58
notice to improve 10

O levels 9
Ofsted inspection framework 8, 37, 38
Ofsted report 44
"outstanding", Ofsted judgements 11, 37, 76–7
outstanding governance 76–7

parent directors 19

parent governors 13, 60
Parent Support Advisers 35
parental involvement 26–7
partnership 16–17
pay 32, 72
performance management 11, 23, 31–3
performance tables 27, 44
PISA programme 45
planning 21
policies 28–30
premises management 30
Priority Schools Building Programme 9
prospectus 28, 44
pupil behaviour 38–40
Pupil Premium 26–7, 44

RAISEonline 22, 24–5
reconstitution 13–15, 60
recruitment of governors 58
removal of governors 14
"requires improvement" 10
resignations, timing of 62
resources 23, 82–8

safeguarding 53–5
school development plan 22
School Information Regulations 27, 42, 44
School Teachers Pay and Conditions Document 47, 72
Schools Financial Value Standard 29, 36–7, 72
self-evaluation 12, 21, 42
SEN 22, 42, 52, 58, 70–71
"serious weaknesses" 10, 55
single academy trust 17
small schools 35
special measures 10, 55
sponsor academies 73
sponsor governors 13–14
staff governors 13, 60
studio schools 74

target-setting 23
teaching school 17, 74
term of office, governors' 14
training 46, 49–50, 57
trust schools 74

umbrella trust 17, 18
University Technical Colleges 74

voluntary schools 14, 15, 73
Wales 45–6, 80
well-being 71